The Segregation Factor in the Florida Democratic Gubernatorial Primary of 1956

Helen L. Jacobstein

University of Florida Press / Gainesville / 1972

Library of Congress Cataloging in Publication Data

Jacobstein, Helen L   1925–
    The segregation factor in the Florida Democratic
gubernatorial primary of 1956.
    (University of Florida social sciences monograph
no. 47)
    Based on the author's thesis (M.A.), University of
Miami, 1964.
    Includes bibliographical references.
    1. Segregation–Florida. 2. Negroes–Segregation.
3. Primaries–Florida. I. Title. II. Series:
Florida. University, Gainesville. University of
Florida monographs. Social sciences, no. 47.
E185.93.F5J3   329'.023'75906   72–3302
ISBN 0–8130–0359–8

SERIES DESIGNED BY STANLEY D. HARRIS

MANUFACTURED BY THE
ROSE PRINTING COMPANY, INCORPORATED
TALLAHASSEE, FLORIDA

Acknowledgments

Tнᴇ subject for this study, originally a master's thesis, was first suggested by an observation made by Dr. Charlton W. Tebeau to the effect that the racial course in Florida was set by the voters' choice of the gubernatorial candidate in the 1956 primary. The study which developed was an attempt to prove this hypothesis.

I am most grateful to all the individuals who permitted themselves to be interviewed, Governor Fuller Warren, Father Theodore Gibson, Vaughn Camp, Jr., Bill Baggs, H. E. S. Reeves, and Henry H. Arrington, and to Lloma G. Green, John McDermott, Charles Hesser, and others who granted telephone interviews. Governor Farris Bryant, Governor LeRoy Collins, and General Sumter Lowry sent information in letters. Governor Collins and the University of South Florida Library made the Collins Papers available to me. I am greatly obliged to Dr. Thomas J. Wood who recommended bibliographical sources, provided some figures on election results, and suggested several additions and clarifications in the text. Dr. William B. Munson, chairman of the Social Science Division, and Dr. J. Riis Owre of the University of Miami Graduate School made this study possible by providing a Graduate Assistantship in Social Science. The constant help and encouragement, sage advice, and unending patience of Dr. Charlton Tebeau will be recalled always with grateful appreciation. The responsibility for all opinions or errors is my own. To my ever forbearing husband and children I owe another debt, for without their encouragement it would have been impossible to complete this work.

Thanks must go also to the Graduate School of the University of Florida for making possible the publication of this monograph.

Helen L. Jacobstein

Contents

1. Segregation in the South and in Florida, 1956   3
2. The Florida Political Situation   13
3. Profiles and Platforms   19
4. The Issue of Segregation   27
5. Economic Development and Other Issues   41
6. Campaign Techniques and Tactics   53
7. Sources of Support   57
8. Effects of the Primary   68
Appendix   79

The Segregation Factor in the Florida Democratic Gubernatorial Primary of 1956

1. Segregation in the South and in Florida, 1956

THE FLORIDA Democratic gubernatorial primary of 1956 represented a crucial decision in Florida's racial history. To many, the election may be explained simply in terms of economic factors, and these were unquestionably decisive. Nevertheless, a review of the events prompts consideration of the factors of personality, public relations techniques, and accident in determining the course Florida was to follow after 1956.

Florida's decision to elect a moderate in 1956 was made in the midst of racial agitation by white segregationists throughout the South. This agitation had been growing since World War II. The war had drastically changed the position of the black in the United States. For the first time, he had enough purchasing power to be an important part of the economy. With the mass migration to northern states, he had also begun to vote in numbers large enough to be a determining factor in key city and state elections. With improved education, purchasing power, and voting strength, the blacks mounted a drive for fuller citizenship, under the direction of the National Association for the Advancement of Colored People (NAACP).

The NAACP won its most significant victories in the courts. In 1944, the Supreme Court struck down the white primary in *Smith* v. *Allright*. Thereafter, blacks began to register and vote in significant numbers in Texas and Florida cities and in the border states.

President Truman's program to implement civil rights produced the first rebellion by some white southerners, who walked out of the 1948 Democratic Convention rather than accept a strong civil rights plank. This "Dixiecrat" movement failed to change the 1948 election, but resentment continued to grow against intrusion of federal authority into state management of racial relations. The spark which ignited the flame of open resistance was the Supreme

3

Court decision to desegregate the schools. The Florida gubernatorial primary of 1956 can perhaps best be understood by a consideration of the reaction throughout the South to this decision of 1954. A most ·deceptive calm followed the *Brown v. Topeka Board of Education* decision. In general, little agitation occurred in the South, although White Citizens Councils began to form in Mississippi. People were waiting to see what form implementation of the decision would take. The implementation decree of May 1955, which set no deadline and referred individual cases to the federal district judges, gave segregationists renewed hope that they could place their faith in their native district judges. As Lieutenant Governor Ernest Vandiver of Georgia expressed it, "A 'reasonable time' can be construed as one year or two hundred. . . . Thank God we've got good Federal judges."[1]

But throughout the remainder of 1955, segregationists noted with chagrin that in each case which was decided by a district court, the Supreme Court ruling was upheld. By January 1956, nineteen of these decisions had been handed down. Florida, Arkansas, Tennessee, and Texas school segregation laws were set aside.

The NAACP, sensing that the civil rights movement had finally gained momentum, filed petitions for desegregation with 170 school boards in 17 states. In 1954 seventeen states and the District of Columbia had legally segregated schools. Desegregation in the border states began promptly, so that by early 1956, there were some 256,000 blacks in integrated schools in the South, about 10 per cent of the total school children involved. Nearly all of these were in the border states. Seven states were resisting, Florida among them.[2]

Hugh Douglas Price, in *The Negro and Southern Politics*, established a table ranking the southern and border states according to their southern characteristics, using six criteria: (1) opposition to civil rights as evidenced by support of Thurmond in 1948; (2) loyalty to the Democratic Party in 1924 and 1928; (3) over 20 per cent black population in 1950; (4) Confederate state in 1861; (5) slave state in 1860; (6) required statewide school integration as of May 1954. Florida reacted in "unsouthern" fashion regarding

1. C. Vann Woodward, *The Strange Career of Jim Crow* (New York: Oxford University Press, 1957), pp. 156–58.
2. Bert Collier, "Dixie Must Act on Racial Issue," *Miami Herald*, March 27, 1956, sec. A, p. 1.

the first two criteria, but had all of the other four characteristics. Price accordingly placed Florida in Rank III with Virginia and North Carolina as less southern than first-ranked Mississippi, Alabama, South Carolina, and Louisiana or second-ranked Georgia and Arkansas. Texas and Tennessee were in Rank IV, less southern still because of their lower percentage of black population.[3]

With emphasis on the proportion of black population in the states, Donald Matthews and James Prothro, in their *Negroes and the New Southern Politics*, use similar criteria to classify Florida as one of the six states of what they call the Peripheral South—less distinctively southern than the Deep South states of Alabama, Georgia, Louisiana, Mississippi, and South Carolina.[4]

A Gallup poll in February 1956 indicated that eight out of ten southern whites opposed desegregation of the schools. A breakdown by states revealed that almost 25 per cent of the whites in the border states of Kentucky, Tennessee, Oklahoma, and Texas, where the white-black population ratio was eight-to-one, approved the desegregation decision. In Florida, Virginia, Arkansas, and North Carolina, where blacks constituted about one-fourth of the population, four out of five whites were against the Supreme Court decision. But in the Deep South states of Georgia, Mississippi, Alabama, South Carolina, and Louisiana, with more than a third of the population black, nearly 90 per cent rejected desegregation.[5]

Resistance had begun to solidify throughout the South by early 1956. Race relations deteriorated steadily. White Citizens Councils began to organize, spreading from their original location at Indianola, Mississippi, into Alabama, Texas, Arkansas, Georgia, Florida, and Louisiana. Other resistance groups formed also; by March 1956 there were forty-six such organizations.[6] The Federation of Ku Klux Klans gained new life, as did a newer National States Rights Party. But the White Citizens Councils, making an appeal to a more sophisticated, respectable, representative group, became the most powerful in the movement.[7] On April 7,

3. (New York: New York University Press, 1957), pp. 8–9, Table I.
4. (New York: Harcourt, Brace and World, 1966), p. 169.
5. John M. Fenton, "Eight Out of Ten Whites in South Speak Up Against Integration," *Miami Herald*, February 27, 1956, state ed., sec. A, p. 1.
6. Collier, "Dixie Must Act."
7. Elizabeth Deanne Malpass, "Organized Southern Racism Since 1954" (Master's thesis, University of Miami, 1963), pp. 34–35.

1956, a national White Citizens Council of America was founded in New Orleans, representing some 300,000 Citizens Council members in eleven states.[8]

This movement used economic and social reprisals as its primary weapons. Blacks who signed desegregation petitions or who otherwise supported integration were dismissed from their jobs and denied credit by stores and banks. White integrationists also lost jobs or found their businesses boycotted. In many communities it became unwise for a person even to suggest that he might favor gradual integration.[9]

Economic boycott was a two-way weapon. Blacks at last had a considerable degree of purchasing power, and they proceeded to use it. February 1956 was the month of the historic Montgomery bus boycott, led by the Reverend Martin Luther King, Jr., in a campaign of nonviolent resistance.[10]

Some individual cases of violence against blacks occurred in the South at this time. Generally, violence was eschewed by the resistance groups. The first riot in connection with the admission of a black to a previously all-white school occurred on the campus of the University of Alabama over the admission of Autherine Lucy. Moderates and liberals became alarmed and appealed to the North for patience. But the segregationists had gained the initiative, and they managed to change the climate of opinion in most parts of the South so materially that the white liberals and moderates were on the defensive thereafter. As one newspaperman phrased it, "The middle ground is dwindling between the never and the now."[11]

The temptation to make political capital out of the issue was too great for the opportunists. Southern office-holders who formerly had been moderate on the racial question now found themselves pushed into a more extreme position.

On the national scene, Senator Harry Byrd of Virginia assumed leadership of the segregationists in Congress, calling for "massive resistance" against desegregation. Tremendous pressure was used upon the southern congressmen to sign the "Declaration of Constitutional Principles" of March 12, 1956, the so-called Southern

8. Hodding Carter III, *The South Strikes Back* (New York: Doubleday and Company, Inc., 1959), p. 70.

9. Nixon Smiley, "Southerners Deem Violence Unlikely," *Miami Herald*, May 8, 1956, sec. A, p. 2.

10. *Miami Herald*, February 23, 1956, sec. A, p. 2.

11. Collier, "Dixie Must Act."

Manifesto. It has been alleged that most of these congressmen signed it reluctantly after its inflammatory language had been toned down by Senators Spessard Holland and Price Daniels.[12] The only senators who refused to sign it were Kefauver and Gore of Tennessee. Lyndon Johnson of Texas, as majority leader, most conveniently was not asked to sign. Few southern representatives outside the border states had the temerity to refuse.

The two congressmen from North Carolina who did refuse promptly went down to defeat in the 1956 primary.[13] Politicians who refused to jump on the racist bandwagon were generally casualties in the elections that followed. Incumbent Governor "Kissing Jim" Folsom of Alabama was defeated almost three to one in a contest for the position of national committeeman. He himself declared that he couldn't be elected dogcatcher in Alabama at that time. Folsom, though an avowed segregationist, so aroused the extremists by his "soft attitude" that the White Citizens Councils threatened to have him impeached.[14]

In Louisiana, a group of Catholic legislators made plans to prevent the integration of Louisiana's Catholic schools, despite Archbishop Joseph Rummel's pastoral letter.[15]

In Georgia, the President Emeritus of the Georgia State College for Women, Dr. Guy H. Wells, spoke at a Negro college and advocated integration. Governor Marvin Griffin promptly revoked his honorary title and the State Board of Education recommended unanimously that his monthly pension be cut off.[16]

Throughout the South, pressure mounted for additional legislation to circumvent the 1954 decision. The segregationists had little success in Kentucky, where Louisville continued preparations for large-scale integration of its schools. In Tennessee, Governor Frank G. Clement refused to call a special session of the legislature to adopt an interposition resolution. The Tennessee senators, Gore and Kefauver, were equally firm in resisting such pressure. But these were border states with relatively small black populations. The rest of the South was overcome by the wave of demands for new legislation. As John Temple Graves, *Birmingham Post-Herald*

12. Drew Pearson, "Senator Holland Toned Down Manifesto," *Tampa Sunday Tribune*, March 18, 1956, sec. A, p. 30.
13. Woodward, p. 168.
14. *Tampa Sunday Tribune*, March 11, 1956, sec. A, p. 19.
15. *Miami News*, February 2, 1956, sec. B, p. 9.
16. Ibid., March 15, 1956, sec. B, p. 8.

syndicated columnist, told a Miami audience, "The Supreme Court . . . has tortured the Constitution. The South will torture the Supreme Court decision."[17] In an article for the Associated Press, a southerner returning home to Alabama wrote of social affairs he attended where well-educated middle-class people calmly discussed the possibility of secession.[18]

Considering the emotional setting, it was only to be expected that the idea of interposition would be revived. James J. Kilpatrick, editor of the *Richmond News-Leader*, began a campaign advocating the use of the interposition doctrine, the interposing of the sovereignty of the state against federal encroachment upon the states' reserved powers, or, in other words, nullification of the federal action. His editorials came to the attention of officials searching for means of resistance. By February 1956, the Virginia, Alabama, and Georgia legislatures had adopted interposition resolutions.[19]

CLIMATE IN FLORIDA REGARDING SEGREGATION

"In urbanization may be found a major explanation of Florida's relative unconcern about the Negro. While the state's politics is by no means free of Negro-baiting, the dominant attitude on the race question is comparatively mild."[20]

At the beginning of 1956, Florida was one of the four states with no public school integration at any level. However, the U.S. Supreme Court had ruled in 1954 in Flordia *ex rel Virgil Hawkins* v. *Board of Control* that forty-eight-year-old Virgil Hawkins, a black public relations official at Bethune-Cookman College, must be admitted to the University of Florida Law School. The case then returned to the Florida Supreme Court, which ruled in October 1955 that the Florida segregation statutes were void. However, the court ordered a survey made to decide whether Hawkins could be admitted to the Law School without creating "political mischief." The court set May 31 as the deadline for completion of the survey by the state Board of Control.[21]

17. "Integration Progress in 'Core Area' Is Called Unsatisfactory," *Southern School News* 2 (January 1956): 15.
18. Rem Price, "Southerner Returned after Long Absence Feels Tragedy Building up in the Mental Attitude on Race," *Tampa Morning Tribune*, March 19, 1956, p. 19.
19. *Florida Times Union*, February 19, 1956, p. 25.
20. V. O. Key, Jr., *Southern Politics in State and Nation* (New York: Alfred A. Knopf, 1949), p. 85.
21. *Miami Herald*, February 3, 1956, sec. B, p. 11.

The Board of Control, which supervised higher education, prepared a questionnaire with the help of the Attorney-General's office. This was mailed out to 62,000 alumni, students, and parents of the University of Florida, Florida State University, and Florida Agricultural and Mechanical College for Negroes, and to high school seniors who would be the incoming freshman class. The groups were all asked whether they favored immediate integration, whether there should be a reasonable period of adjustment, whether integration should be delayed as long as legally possible, or whether it should never occur in Florida. A number of other related questions were also asked.[22]

The preliminary results of the poll were used by Attorney-General Richard Ervin on March 12 in petitioning the United States Supreme Court for a rehearing of the Hawkins case. Ervin contended that Hawkins' admission would be a "serious disruption of the university system in Florida."[23]

	Students	Parents
admit Negroes now	22.39%	9.04%
never admit Negroes	21.04%	41.62%
delay as long as possible	14.01%	23.98%
favoring reasonable period of adjustment	41.45%	24.10%
would transfer daughters from integrated school		32.29%

A petition signed by 225 University of Florida students pledging themselves to welcome any new student only irritated the segregationists, as did a similar statement made previously by University of Florida faculty members.[24] Crosses were burned on the University of Florida campus to protest the petition. A group of Tallahassee area residents petitioned the state Board of Control to fire some fifty University of Florida professors who favored integration.[25]

The likelihood of an imminent break in the Florida color line, combined with occurrences in the other southern states, radically

22. Ibid., February 11, 1956, sec. A, p. 12.
23. Florida Times Union, April 4, 1956, p. 16.
24. Tampa Morning Tribune, March 23, 1956, sec. A, p. 19.
25. Florida Times Union, February 17, 1956, p. 22.

changed the racial atmosphere during the three months of the gubernatorial primary campaign.[26]

Fred Kent, chairman of the state Board of Control, spoke prior to the campaign of his opposition to integration but said, "I, like other officials of Florida, have swallowed the bitter pill of necessity." He added, "In practically every other state, pandemonium reigns. In Florida alone have we put reason ahead of what we would call righteous anger."[27] Kent, a few months later, was proposing open defiance of the Court.[28]

Attorney-General Richard Ervin had filed a brief in 1954 proposing a theory of "gradualism" in implementing integration. Ervin in 1956, with segregationist Representative Prentiss Pruitt opposing him for re-election, radically changed his position. He proposed a special session of the legislature to deal with the segregation problem immediately. By May he had gone so far as to propose consideration of the Virginia plan, which provided for repeal of the compulsory school attendance laws, offered grants-in-aid to parents sending children to private segregated schools, and permitted local option on the abolition of the public school system.[29]

Senator Spessard Holland said in 1954, "No matter how much we don't like it, or the fact we don't want it, we must not have a false idea of its seriousness. It is going to be the law."[30] However, two years later, on the national television program "Today," he spoke of possible methods of evasion, among them, "discretion in the confirmation of federal judges." He listed as a last resort the closing of the public schools.[31] Holland, according to Florida political analyst Allen Morris, had previously exhibited an uncanny ability to judge latent public opinion.[32] His reversal of position was a good indication of the shifting political winds.

EXTENT OF INTEGRATION IN FLORIDA

Florida in early 1956 retained nearly all the Jim Crow aspects of the Deep South. The most significant exception to the pattern was

26. Allen Morris, "Segregation Shelves Personalities Issue in Governor's Contest," *Miami News*, March 18, 1956, sec. A, p. 1.
27. *Tampa Morning Tribune*, January 26, 1956, p. 14.
28. *Miami Herald*, May 1, 1956, street ed., sec. B, p. 1.
29. *Florida Times Union*, May 17, 1956, p. 24.
30. Bert Collier, "Florida Racial About-Face Performed without Hysteria," *Miami Herald*, April 4, 1956, sec. B, p. 3.
31. *Florida Times Union*, March 13, 1956, p. 19.
32. "Segregation Shelves Personalities Issue in Governor's Contest."

the relatively large black voter registration: 128,437 Democrats and 9,098 Republicans, or about 37.5 per cent of the 1950 adult black population. Black registration was still discouraged in rural North Florida, especially in most of the counties situated between the Apalachicola and Suwannee rivers, which comprised the old Black Belt or former plantation economy of Florida. But in most urban areas, and in many rural communities as well, there was no bar to black registration and voting.[33]

Pressure for integration of some public facilities was increasing in cities with predominantly "northern" populations. These pressures were exerted by the blacks themselves, by church groups, and by other white liberal elements. The Ministerial Association in Fort Lauderdale endorsed formation of an interracial council leading to desegregation.[34] In Volusia County, the white and black ministerial associations of the Halifax and Daytona Beach areas merged, and interracial services were held.[35]

The Daytona buses had been integrated for five years, although technically the blacks were supposed to load from the rear and whites from the front. At rush hours, the buses were completely desegregated in the middle, without complaint. Five black drivers, who had been employed for fifteen to eighteen years, were retained in the consolidated system.[36]

The federally operated Tinker Elementary School at MacDill Field in Tampa admitted a black child on January 2, 1956. This, according to the *Tampa Tribune*, "attracted no attention whatever."[37] Tinker had been a county-run school until June 1955, when the national government assumed operation.

Miami, the least southern of the Florida cities, had made some beginnings toward integration. Many special church meetings were integrated. A few churches had black members. Some hotels, restaurants, and night clubs admitted blacks (usually as convention members or entertainers).[38] The convention business in Dade County was a sizable part of the tourist industry. National con-

33. Hugh Douglas Price, *The Negro and Southern Politics* (New York: New York University Press, 1957), pp. 34–40.
34. *Miami Herald*, May 3, 1956, Broward ed., p. 6.
35. *Miami News*, March 6, 1956, sec. B, p. 2.
36. *Miami Herald*, April 26, 1956, sec. B, p. 1.
37. *Tampa Morning Tribune*, February 2, 1956, sec. A, p. 17.
38. Jack Bell, "Miami Desegregating Now in Some Ways," *Miami Herald*, March 25, 1956, sec. G, p. 4.

ventions at times refused to hold meetings where black members would not be accommodated, so rather than lose the business, the hotels quietly admitted the black convention members.

In industry, a little progress toward integration had been made, but changes on a large scale were obviously on the way. "Negro and white are working together in many of our plants, side by side with no ill feeling that I'm aware of," said Otis Dunan, president of the Greater Miami Manufacturers' Association. At Miami International Airport, one of the major aviation companies, which depended upon government contracts for the major part of its business, had more than 100 blacks working side-by-side with whites, six of the blacks in highly skilled jobs.[39]

Labor unions, though still segregated, were just beginning to integrate. The Congress of Industrial Organizations was reportedly more favorable to integration, with a black trustee on its state board, than the American Federation of Labor, which had a black vice-president but was reputed to be segregationist. Unexpectedly, the unions with the most integration (with one exception) were those in the northern and western parts of the state: in Pinellas and Hillsborough counties and even in Panama City and Apalachicola. The only completely integrated union in Dade, Local 643 of the Hebrew Butchers, Workmen, and Allied Trades Union, was the one exception; the unions on the lower Gold Coast were resisting integration.[40]

With these few exceptions, Floridians were segregated in schools, churches, public facilities, job opportunities, and almost all other significant ways. The countervailing forces for segregation and integration were at work in Florida before and during the election period. In the face of mounting tension and frustration over the race question, the integrationists were pushed to the defensive, remaining there until freed by federal action and gradually cooling tempers.

39. John F. Bonner, "Industrial Integration," *Miami Herald*, April 29, 1956, sec. D, p. 11.

40. Bryan Donaldson, "Labor Still Segregated," *Miami Herald*, May 2, 1956, sec. C, p. 1.

2. The Florida Political Situation

FLORIDA is not only unbossed, it is also unled."[1] V. O. Key, Jr., could have been describing the state in 1956 rather than 1949. He attributed much of Florida's amorphous political situation to the state's geography as well as to its diversity of population and economic interests. The 800-mile distance from Pensacola to Key West has been a great deterrent to political organization.

Perhaps more significant was its heterogeneous population. Florida had native "Crackers" in North Florida, Cubans in Tampa (and to a lesser extent in 1956 in Miami), Jews in Miami Beach, and Greeks in Tarpon Springs. There were retirees in St. Petersburg, blacks concentrated in Jacksonville, Miami, and some rural northern counties, and, most meaningful of all, huge numbers of immigrants from other states, nearly all of them settled in peninsular Florida. Half of the population was born out of the state.

Vast economic differences existed between rural North Florida, the central citrus belt, the south-central cattle area, and the large urban centers. Even the northern and western rural sections had areas of tourist strips like Panama City, university towns like Tallahassee and Gainesville, and industrial towns. Pensacola, for example, had huge military installations, paper mills, and a nearby $85 million Chemstrand nylon plant.[2] Wide differences divided the urban areas as well. Jacksonville was a leading insurance center as well as a railroad and seaport hub, yet it retained many of the "Old South" attitudes to which Miami and St. Petersburg, populated by new Floridians and concerned with tourism, attached little significance.[3]

Rapid immigration had produced a fluid social and political situ-

1. Key, *Southern Politics in State and Nation*, p. 83.
2. William A. Emerson, Jr., "The Peculiar State of Florida Politics," *Newsweek* 47 (May 7, 1956): 30.
3. William C. Havard and Loren P. Beth, *The Politics of Misrepresentation* (Baton Rouge: Louisiana State University Press, 1962), pp. 20–21.

ation where factions had not had time to develop. The population was estimated to have increased 33 per cent between 1950 and 1956. This population growth was accompanied by a corresponding increase in urbanization, so that by 1956 the urban areas had over 70 per cent of the people.[4]

Urbanization had so shifted voting power that the ten largest counties in 1956 could control a statewide election. The gubernatorial primaries of 1952 and 1954 reflected this dominance. The urban areas tended to have an overwhelming business orientation, particularly because of the weakness of organized labor. Governors Dan McCarty and LeRoy Collins were both inclined toward urban interests and moderate conservatism, advocating governmental reform such as constitutional revision, reapportionment, better schools and highways, and a moderate approach to racial problems.[5]

The huge numbers of transplanted northerners and the great interest in economic development and rapid industrialization were largely responsible for Florida's political dichotomy—presidential Republicanism and Democratic control of state and local government. Republicans had not made a serious attempt to capture state and local offices except in two or three counties and, consequently, one-party rule still prevailed in 1956.

Lack of competition from another party plus the aforementioned factors contributed to Florida's unstructured politics. This relative absence of faction produced a situation where each candidate concerned himself only with his own campaign. One candidate collaborating with another could easily transfer that candidate's enemies to himself, and would leave himself open to the charge of being part of a machine. An outgoing office-holder often was unable to transfer his following to a favored successor, for such endorsement would have left him open to charges of creating a dynasty. Frequently a governor, for example, could not even keep his own following should he subsequently run for the Senate. Spessard Holland was considered a rare political phenomenon for accomplishing such a feat in 1946.[6] Factions, where they actually existed, constantly shifted in such a political atmosphere.

The cabinet in Florida was exceedingly powerful. Cabinet mem-

4. Allen Morris (comp.), *The Florida Handbook* (Tallahassee: Peninsular Publishing Co., 1957), pp. 321–22.
5. Havard and Beth, p. 20.   6. Key, p. 102.

bers, in contrast to the governor, could succeed themselves in office. Most frequently, they ran unopposed. By 1956 Nathan Mayo, the incumbent Commissioner of Agriculture, had served in that capacity for thirty-three years. The Secretary of State, R. A. Gray, had been in office since 1930. Because of this security of tenure, cabinet members tended to build up their own influence with the legislature. Their independence of the governor combined with their tenure weakened the executive office.

The governor's position with the legislature was also relatively powerless. The Florida legislature, because of malapportionment, had been representative largely of rural North Florida. The governor, often elected statewide by the preponderantly urban South Florida vote, frequently had little control over the legislature beyond patronage, the veto, and his own persuasive powers. The constitutional prohibition against a second consecutive four-year term for the governor reduced the effectiveness of the patronage factor on the legislature.

Such factors as personality and public relations techniques were disproportionately important for candidates because of the lack of party and factional leadership. Personality differences became all important in the gubernatorial elections before 1956 because of the absence of overwhelmingly important issues. Candidates argued over local law enforcement, the best road-building plan, or taxes, but ideological differences were often undiscernible. Prosperity and immigration had made Florida unreceptive to the economic liberal, personified by Senator Claude Pepper.[7]

A number of events which had occurred in previous administrations were profoundly influencing Florida politics in 1956. The Fuller Warren administration (1949–53) had gained a reputation of indifference to gambling and racketeering, particularly because of Warren's refusal to testify before the Kefauver Committee investigating rackets.

Dan McCarty had been elected in 1952 on a platform dedicated to strict law enforcement, industrial expansion, and better schools and highways. He suffered a heart attack a month after his inauguration and died in September 1953. Florida had no lieutenant governor until the 1968 constitutional revision. The president of the Senate, Charley Johns, succeeded McCarty as acting governor until the next election, in accordance with Florida law.

7. Morris, "Segregation Shelves Personalities Issue in Governor's Contest."

Johns was leader of the Senate majority from rural North Florida. He reversed most of McCarty's programs and fired his appointees. All the members of the State Road Board and the State Racing Commission were replaced with Johns' supporters. Public indignation against Johns, especially in urban South Florida, was extreme. Johns ran again in 1954 for the remaining two years of McCarty's term. LeRoy Collins, who pledged himself to carry out McCarty's program, ran second to Johns in the first primary. Brailey Odham, McCarty's adversary in 1952 and third man in the 1954 primary, threw his support to Collins. Odham's supporters followed his example, for Collins gained almost as many votes in the second primary as Odham had received, thus defeating Charley Johns 380,000 to 314,000. The vote was plainly along sectional lines. Johns won thirty-four of the thirty-six North Florida counties. Collins carried populous South Florida by a wide margin, but in North Florida won only his own Leon and adjacent Jefferson counties.[8]

The sectional battle for reapportionment in the 1955 legislature left its scars. An open cleavage between large and small counties developed over the unresolved reapportionment issue. The North Florida counties refused to relinquish any substantial power despite the constitutional requirement that they reapportion according to specified criteria. Members of the Pork Chop Gang, as the dominant rural North Florida faction of the legislature was called, openly resented Collins' appeal over their heads to the rest of the state. Their resentment carried over to other issues, and from that time on they stood as a more or less permanent faction against urban interests.[9] Thus, while permanent factions were almost nonexistent in most of Florida, the Pork Chop Gang had emerged as a functional one by the time of the 1956 primary.

Special interests played a disproportionately important role in Florida politics. For almost twenty years, Ed Ball, representative of the huge Du Pont Florida interests, was a dominant figure in Florida politics. He had pressed for a sales tax for many years, and finally succeeded during the Warren administration in getting one passed. He had contributed to Warren's campaign.[10] Road con-

8. Price, *The Negro and Southern Politics*, p. 98.

9. Havard and Beth, p. 58.

10. Martin Waldron, "The Establishment: Rural 'Pork Chop Gang' Rules the Capital Roost," *Miami Herald*, February 18, 1964, sec. A, p. 20.

tractors, liquor distributors, and racetrack operators were also major contributors to political campaigns. They and innumerable others maintained well-financed lobbyists and exerted considerable power in government.

In the months before the 1956 primary campaign, much speculation centered around whether Governor LeRoy Collins would be declared eligible to succeed himself. A number of Collins' supporters considered running if he were ruled ineligible or if the Supreme Court delayed ruling until after the qualifying date. John McCarty, Dan McCarty's brother, who was proxy governor for six months during the latter's illness, was one of those mentioned, as was former United States Representative William Lantaff of Miami, Brailey Odham of Sanford, former Senator Henry Baynard of St. Petersburg, and House Speaker Thomas E. (Ted) David of Hollywood.[11] In addition to Collins' backers, former Comptroller C. M. Gay of Orlando said that he was seriously considering the gubernatorial contest, and friends of former Acting Governor Charley Johns said that concern over integration might motivate him to try once again.[12]

State Representative C. Farris Bryant had been preparing for the governor's campaign for three years and was the first serious candidate to announce, followed by Lt. Gen. Sumter Lowry and then Fuller Warren, the former governor. Warren's candidacy was viewed as the most serious threat to Collins. His friends said that his organization was practically intact. John McDermott of the *Miami Herald,* talking of Warren's imminent announcement, predicted that Johns' supporters would back him, and that his native rural Northwest Florida would give him a heavy majority as would populous Duval County, where he had lived for twenty years.[13] Even Warren's bitterest enemies respected his ability and influence. Brailey Odham said, "Warren is a definite threat. He will be minus the power of the governor's office, which Johns had, but he will have the gratitude of many of his followers with whom he dealt intimately while he served as Governor. Fuller possesses the ability to appeal to the masses of the voters—to convince them that he's the best friend they can have in office."[14] Bryant was not

11. *Miami Herald,* March 2, 1956, sec. A, p. 1.
12. *Florida Times Union,* February 19, 1956, p. 22.
13. "Warren Runs for Governor," *Miami Herald,* February 17, 1956, street ed., sec. A, p. 1.
14. *Miami News,* February 5, 1956, sec. A, p. 4.

rated much of a chance if Collins were ruled eligible. Bryant's timing in choosing a year when incumbent Collins was running was considered a mistake, particularly since he was at the height of his influence and popularity in 1953 when he was speaker.[15] Bryant's appeal was thought to be to substantially the same voters who were expected to support Collins. At the same time, it was believed that Warren would gain strength if Bryant could siphon off enough of Collins' votes.[16] Even as late as March 22, Warren was still rated Collins' chief opposition.[17]

Lowry's candidacy was not lightly disregarded by political observers. Charles Hesser of the *Miami News* predicted, "As the campaign wears on, Lowry will promise more and more and demand more and more from his adversaries." He went on to warn those who scoffed at Lowry's candidacy that in 1916, Sidney J. Catts won election on an anti-Catholic and prohibition platform over four opponents. Resentment over integration now, Hesser speculated, might be deeper than religious prejudice in 1916.[18]

The Florida Supreme Court finally ruled on March 5, one day before the end of the qualifying period, that Collins was eligible to run again because he hadn't served a full four-year term.[19] Collins supporters were jubilant, the other candidates correspondingly disgruntled. Collins, as incumbent, was considered the man to beat. As governor, he had opportunities to act on issues while the others could only make promises. He could appear at state functions and before organizations and could get news coverage not available to the other candidates. He also had the inside track in tapping the sources of contribution money.

At the close of the 1955 legislature, it had appeared that taxes would be the primary issue in the 1956 gubernatorial campaign. However, continued prosperity brought an unanticipated collection of taxes, thus eliminating it as an issue.[20] The most obvious issue to fill the vacuum, considering the experiences of the rest of the South, was integration.

15. John McDermott, "Three Candidates Look Alike," *Miami Herald*, March 18, 1956, sec. G, p. 3.

16. *Miami News*, February 5, 1956, sec. A, p. 4.

17. McDermott, "Three Candidates."

18. "Campaign Issue: Segregation," *Miami News*, February 5, 1956, sec. C, p. 2.

19. *Florida Times Union*, March 6, 1956, p. 18.

20. Hendrix Chandler, "Tax Issue Fades as Governorship Campaign Issue," *Tampa Sunday Tribune*, February 5, 1956, sec. A, p. 8.

3. Profiles and Platforms

LeRoy Collins was an example of the poor boy who made good. The son of a Tallahassee neighborhood grocer, he worked as a delivery boy and stock clerk in another grocery for his tuition at the Eastman School of Business in Poughkeepsie, New York, and as a shipping clerk and bank teller to pay his way to law school at Cumberland University. He was elected state representative from Leon County in 1932 at the age of twenty-five, remaining in the House until 1940 when he was elected state senator. With time out for war service in the Navy, Collins served in the Senate until 1954.[1] In 1953, he was named "most valuable" senator in the *St. Petersburg Times* poll of the press and "most valuable legislator" in the Allen Morris poll of legislators.[2]

Though a native of Northwest Florida, in the legislature Collins was generally identified with the progressive forces who advocated constitutional revision, better schools, women's rights, and aid to the disabled, deaf, and blind. He led in the campaign to outlaw slot machines[3] and in 1953 was one of the chief Senate proponents of the full Florida turnpike.[4]

Collins had been a personal friend of the late Governor Dan McCarty. He ran for governor in 1954 to fill the remaining two years of McCarty's term, opposing Acting Governor Charley Johns and Brailey Odham, Sanford businessman. Collins' efforts to secure administrative reorganization, allocation of additional funds for buying highway rights of way, and other items in his program were largely frustrated in the 1955 legislature because of the acrimony which developed over the reapportionment issue. He was

1. Morris, *The Florida Handbook* (1959 ed.), pp. 106–17.
2. Ibid., p. 141.
3. *Miami Herald*, editorial, May 7, 1956, sec. A, p. 6.
4. Ibid., May 6, 1956, sec. G, p. 1.

criticized by his own supporters for his failure to use patronage and restriction of road construction to club recalcitrant legislators into line.[5] Many believed that Collins could have achieved more progress simply by making personal appeals to several wavering legislators or by bribing them with public displays of regard in front of the press or newsreel cameras.

He made a great effort to identify himself with business, particularly by encouraging new industry to settle in Florida. Collins' image in the state press and with the Chambers of Commerce, especially in South Florida, remained untarnished despite his legislative rebuffs.

His personality and family life were certainly most effective in presenting the proper image. He was married to a descendant of the territorial governor Richard Keith Call. He and his wife had four children, including a little girl who in 1956 was a most appealing subject for newspaper photographers. Collins himself was young (forty-seven), tall, slim, and handsome. He presented an air of sincerity and urbanity, which was effectively transmitted to the public, for he was skilled in radio and television speaking.

Fuller Warren, governor of Florida from 1949 to 1953, was a native of Blountstown in rural Northwest Florida. He attended the University of Florida and received his law degree, like Collins, from Cumberland University. He was a political prodigy, for he was elected to serve his native Calhoun County in the state legislature when he was only twenty-one, while he was still at the University of Florida. He moved to Jacksonville, practiced law, and served three terms on the city council and one term in the legislature as a representative of Duval County. He was defeated as a gubernatorial candidate in 1940, running third with 17.3 per cent of the vote, but in 1948, after war service in the Navy, he defeated Dan McCarty in the second primary with a margin of 23,000 votes.[6] He ran strongest in rural Northwest Florida, where he campaigned with a hillbilly band playing "Roly-Poly."[7] Warren was considered less conservative than McCarty, picking up considerable labor and urban black support, as well as the remnant Populist vote of North Florida.[8]

5. Havard and Beth, The Politics of Misrepresentation, pp. 57–59.
6. Morris, 1959 ed., p. 204.
7. Morris, Appendix to Fuller Warren, How to Win in Politics (Tallahassee: Peninsular Publishing Company, 1949), p. 169.
8. Key, Southern Politics in State and Nation, pp. 95–100.

Warren's administration aroused considerable controversy. On the one hand, a number of major improvement projects were begun during his term of office. He promoted the fencing of the open range, road-building, unmasking of the Ku Klux Klan, and attracting of industry. He had run on an anti–sales tax plank, but once in office, he called the legislature into special session in 1949, after their failure to make the necessary appropriations, and supported the limited sales tax which was passed. It was noted that Ed Ball, Du Pont brother-in-law and long a law unto himself in Florida politics, had contributed to Warren's campaign and had promoted the sales tax for many years. Warren battled constantly with the state newspapers. The Kefauver Crime Investigating Committee discovered that Warren's campaign had been mostly financed by three individuals: Jacksonville financier Louis Wolfson, who gave over $150,000, citrus and real estate investor C. V. Griffin, who contributed over $154,000, and horse and dog track official William H. (Big Bill) Johnson, who gave over $100,000.[9] The Florida newspapers seized upon the revelations with glee. Warren's refusal to respond to a subpoena from the Kefauver Committee which was investigating organized crime in Florida created additional controversy.

Warren, divorced before his term as governor, married a young California beauty queen while in office. They moved to Miami Beach on completion of his term and Warren practiced law in Dade County. In 1956, he was fifty years old, silver-haired, and personable. He was a man of considerable charm and persuasiveness, friendly and genial, a skilled orator with an unmistakable North Florida accent, a tremendous vocabulary, and a quick wit, never at a loss for the apt retort. Warren was generally categorized as a "Cracker" politician, whose effectiveness in Florida was minimized by the urbanity of the so-called Chamber of Commerce type of candidate, exemplified by Senator George Smathers or LeRoy Collins.[10]

Lieutenant General Sumter Lowry, retired, was from Tampa. He had attended Virginia Military Institute, where he won the Cincinnati award for outstanding achievement, but the Virginia Military Institute education gave him no advantage in the regular army, and after several frustrating years, he resigned to go into

9. *Tampa Morning Tribune*, February 26, 1956, p. 30.
10. Havard and Beth, p. 28.

business.[11] He was in the National Guard for thirty-five years, serving overseas in both world wars and receiving the state and national distinguished service medals. He helped organize the American Legion and was a former state commander.[12]

Lowry was exceedingly successful as a businessman. He was chairman of the board of the Gulf Life Insurance Company. He later sold a major part of his Gulf Life holdings to the Murchison interests of Texas, but he remained on the board. Lowry had also served as chairman of the board of both Bushnell Steel Company of Jacksonville and Cuban American Metals Distributors, Inc., of Havana.[13]

Lowry first entered the Florida political arena in the late 1940s, when he attacked the United Nations and the World Federalist Movement. The local World Federalists called for his resignation as commanding general of the Fifty-first National Guard Division. He refused to resign, and renewed his attacks on the United Nations. He joined the Republicans in 1952, and became regional director in Eisenhower's Florida campaign.[14] A month before announcing his candidacy, Lowry spoke before the Duval County Democratic Executive Committee, where he vehemently denounced integration as part of a Communist conspiracy to destroy the moral fibre of the nation by creating a "mongrel" race incapable of preventing a Red take-over.[15]

Lowry was widowed and remarried. He had two married children from his first marriage and a daughter from his second. In 1956, he was sixty-two years old, bald, wore glasses, had a rather forbidding expression, and lacked the appeal and charm of his rivals. He appeared to have an "overwhelmingly military attitude toward everything."[16] Though sometimes criticized as a fanatic and an extremist, he seemed to have his emotions well under control.

C. Farris Bryant (he dropped the C. for his next campaign) of Ocala was generally conceded to be one of the ablest legislators in Florida. He was a graduate of the University of Florida and

11. Interview with Vaughn Camp, Jr., Lowry's nephew and aide during the campaign, February 24, 1964.
12. Paul Wilder, "Gen. Sumter Lowry: Prophet of the Red Peril," *Tampa Morning Tribune*, February 19, 1961, sec. E, p. 1.
13. *Florida Times Union*, March 23, 1956, p. 20.
14. Wilder, "Gen. Sumter Lowry."
15. Price, *The Negro and Southern Politics*, pp. 85–86.
16. Interview with Vaughn Camp, Jr.

of Harvard Law School. He was elected to the state legislature from Marion County, and was still serving in 1956. He was selected "most outstanding member of the House" by the *St. Petersburg Times* poll in 1949, 1953, and 1955, and "most valuable legislator" by the Allen Morris poll in 1953,[17] when he was speaker. In 1952, Bryant had been chairman of the Florida delegation to the Democratic National Convention, championing Senator Richard Russell of Georgia. Generally, Bryant and Collins had supported many of the same governmental reforms and in 1955, Bryant had backed most of Collins' program. However, they split sharply over the reapportionment issue.[18] It had been assumed for three years that Bryant was grooming himself for the governorship.[19]

In 1956 Bryant was forty-one years old, married, and the father of three daughters. Though bald, his appearance was attractive, his manner convincing, and his speaking ability considerable. Harvard had done little to modify his heavy southern accent, an asset in Florida politics. Bryant has been criticized for lacking warmth. His manner was more dignified than that of either Collins or Warren. He was neither as colorful a personality as Warren nor as handsome and appealing as Collins.

Two minor candidates also paid the $1,000 qualifying fees. Peasley Streets, a Lake Park (Palm Beach County) constable, was a former Warren administration employee, having been a Motor Vehicle Department inspector and a member of the state Game and Fresh Water Fish Commission. He was an unsuccessful candidate for the state Railroad and Public Utilities Commission in 1952.[20] Streets declared himself in favor of integration because it was the law of the land. It was alleged that Streets entered the race to aid Warren by drawing off black votes from Collins.[21] He neither campaigned actively nor received any significant support. The other minor candidate, W. B. (Bill) Price, a fifty-six-year-old Jacksonville used-car dealer, apparently paid the filing fee to seek vindication at the polls for his allegedly wrongful commitment to the state mental hospital. He had previously filed suits against two Florida legislators for refusing to

17. Morris, *The Florida Handbook*, 1959 ed., p. 141.
18. *Miami News*, March 12, 1956, sec. A, p. 2, final ed.
19. *Miami Herald*, May 6, 1956, sec. G, p. 1.
20. Ibid., February 23, 1956, sec. B, p. 1.
21. Price, p. 100.

introduce bills to have the state pay him for his improper confinement at Chattahoochee.[22]

Collins declared that constitutional revision and clean, honest, economical, and efficient government were Florida's greatest needs. He favored periodic, automatic reapportionment based upon population changes, with withdrawal of this power from the legislature should it fail to reapportion. He favored a Department of Finance, consolidation of the major state tax-collecting functions into a division of revenue, and centralization of state purchasing into a division of purchasing.[23] He favored an elective successor to the governor, prohibition of secret meetings of the Senate, home rule, reorganization of the courts, a state department of labor, better educational facilities, improved labor, health, and welfare standards, and conservation of natural resources. Unlike his opponents, he made no mention of the race problem at the beginning of the campaign.[24]

Collins ran on his record as governor, placing greatest emphasis upon his record of attracting industry to Florida, and of creating a favorable national image of Florida as a stable, progressive, well-managed state receptive to business needs. He stressed his role in obtaining better schools, welfare benefits, and roads, and cited his administration record of integrity, better law enforcement, and economy.

Warren ran on a forty-seven-point "platform" and on the record of his administration. He stressed his opposition as governor to illegal gambling and to the sales tax.[25] He cited support that he gave for the first Florida turnpike, livestock fencing, taste-test citrus code, flood control and reforestation, school improvement, and welfare appropriations. He also credited his administration with bringing industry into the state. Warren proposed increasing the $5,000 homestead exemption to $10,000. He endorsed the Sixty-Seven Senator Amendment which was to be voted upon statewide in November. Warren also advocated more roads, bridges, a "factory for every county, stricter law enforcement, a Supreme Court judge from Dade County when the

22. *Miami Herald*, May 6, 1956, sec. G, p. 5.
23. Florida League of Women Voters, 1956 Gubernatorial Questionnaire.
24. *Meet LeRoy Collins*, undated campaign brochure.
25. League of Women Voters Questionnaire.

next vacancy occurs, and constitutional revision." He placed great emphasis upon his residence in Dade County, upon the fact that if he were elected he would be the first governor from Dade, and upon support of the home rule amendment for Dade County. However, his first plank was a pledge to "do everything in my power to maintain segregation."[26]

Bryant placed constitutional revision and economy as the state's prime needs. Regarding segregation, he proposed joining with other southern governors to work out a program to maintain it without force or violence.[27] He stressed his support of economy measures, improved schools, flood control, and the full Florida turnpike, and his opposition to quickie divorces, the sales tax, and legalized gambling.[28] Bryant also advocated a lieutenant governor and the Sixty-Seven Senator Plan. Attacking Collins' failure to implement his 1954 platform, Bryant promised better leadership which would result in cooperation from the legislature.[29] He cited the need for tolerance and understanding between the large and small counties and the various sections of the state, in order to end sectionalism.[30]

Lowry began his campaign on a single plank, a "one-hundred per cent segregation platform," based primarily on the use of interposition. When questioned regarding other issues, he insisted that segregation was "the greatest issue before the people in the last 100 years."[31] Some of his replies on other issues were:

Question: What sort of reapportionment plan do you advocate?

Answer: That's a matter for the legislature to decide. The governor has no power in that.

Question: Are you in favor of the sixty-seven senator constitutional amendment?

Answer: I have no position on that. The people will vote on it and I'll carry out my duties.

26. John McDermott, "Sixty-Seven Man Senate Blasted," *Miami Herald,* February 22, 1956, sec. A, p. 1.
27. *Miami Herald,* March 3, 1956, sec. A, p. 5.
28. League of Women Voters Questionnaire.
29. *Tampa Sunday Tribune,* March 11, 1956, p. 16.
30. *Tampa Morning Tribune,* February 11, 1956, p. 14.
31. Bob Delaney, " 'Interposition Will Stop It,' Says Lowry of Integration," *Miami News,* March 27, 1956, sec. B, p. 11.

Question: Do you think Florida's constitution needs revising and if so, in what way or ways?

Answer: When I get to be governor, I'll go into that thoroughly.

Question: Are you in favor of having a lieutenant governor in Florida?

Answer: I'll think about it.

Question: Do you think there should be consolidation of the tax collection agencies in the state?

Answer: I'd rather give that very careful thought before answering.

Question: What is your position on homestead exemption?

Answer: I have none.

Question: If state revenue should prove insufficient to meet demands in the next few years, what would you recommend, as governor, to solve the problem?

Answer: I'll make a study of it at that time.

Lowry presented a three-point program to deal with segregation: cooperation with the other southern states to combat federal interference, official leadership by the governor as the state's spokesman, and the resolution of interposition previously mentioned.[32]

32. *Florida Times Union*, February 29, 1956, p. 21.

4. The Issue of Segregation

SUMTER LOWRY set the tone of the gubernatorial campaign on February 1 when he formally announced his candidacy: he charged that Collins had been evasive, Warren silent, and Bryant accepting of integration. He promised that he would provide positive leadership rather than defeatism and "pussy-footing."[1] Each of his opponents, Lowry declared, "has openly or secretly advanced the cause of integration forces and the NAACP."[2] He accused Collins of failing to understand both the threat to the state's customs and his obligation to fight this threat. Collins was willing to "let nature take its course—lull our people to sleep—make integration gradual but final and bring about the ruin of our great state."[3]

The other three hastened to respond, although Warren and Collins had not yet announced their candidacies. Bryant replied, "I don't believe demagoguery and passion on the one hand are going to solve the problem, nor do I believe that wearing the blinders on the other hand is going to solve it."[4] He went on to say, "The problem calls for cool heads, clear minds, and a keen concern for the welfare of all Floridians, black and white."

Collins felt himself obliged to issue a statement through his administrative assistant, Joe Grotegut, saying, "Our leadership has been far more effective than has been the case in many other states in which a great deal more noise and confusion has been generated."[5] He declared his opposition to "defiance of constituted authority" and to "any effort to make political capital out of segregation." Addressing a group of Tampa businessmen the following week, Collins assured them that segregation could be kept

1. *Miami Herald*, February 2, 1956, sec. A, p. 1.
2. Ibid., February 29, 1956, sec. A, p. 2.
3. *Miami News*, February 8, 1956, sec. B, p. 5.
4. Ibid., February 2, 1956, sec. B, p. 5.
5. *Miami Herald*, February 3, 1956, sec. C, p. 1.

"without furor," saying, "Believe me when I say Florida cannot afford an orgy of race conflict and discord."[6]

Warren declared, "I am opposed to mixing of the races and I think Florida public officials should do everything in their power to prevent it."[7] Warren had received a large majority of black votes in 1948 and was generally considered a moderate on the racial question. He did not conspicuously voice objection to introduction of the race issue into the campaign, although speaking of it much later, he said that it had no proper place in the governor's race but that "He [Lowry] thrust it in." Warren's opinion was that it was not properly a state issue but a federal one.[8]

While Collins, Warren, and Bryant either publicly or privately deplored injection of the segregation issue, Lowry mounted the offensive and kept it thereafter, attacking the candidates, the Supreme Court, the NAACP, and the Communist conspiracy. Lowry rejected Collins' contention that Florida's economy would suffer from an all-out fight against integration. On the contrary, the tourist industry would be injured if people found themselves obliged to send their children to mixed schools, playgrounds, or swimming pools. Lowry said of Collins, "He would sell out the children of the state for the dollar bill."[9]

The atmosphere in Florida began to resemble the Deep South more and more. Bill Baggs, the *Miami News* columnist, wrote about a new game in Florida politics played by competing candidates which promised to become more popular than gin rummy: "The name of the game is 'I Love Segregation More Than You Do,' the man with the loudest voice and the most indignant expression wins."[10] In the heat of the campaign a series of incidents involving race relations that might otherwise have passed unnoticed was seized upon for campaign purposes by the candidates. This had the effect of increasing racial tensions. In consequence there were signs that Florida might go the way of other Deep South states in this respect.

The first of these incidents occurred in Lake County as the aftermath of the sensational Groveland rape case of 1949. Four

6. Ibid., February 8, 1956, sec. C, p. 6.
7. Ibid., February 6, 1956, sec. B, p. 1.
8. Interview with Fuller Warren, March 3, 1964.
9. *Miami News*, February 8, 1956, sec. B, p. 8.
10. "Brailey Odham and Segregation," *Miami News*, March 19, 1956, sec. A, p. 19.

blacks had been convicted of raping a seventeen-year-old white housewife. The case had dragged on in the courts for years. In 1952, Sheriff McCall shot two of the defendants in "self-defense," killing one of them and wounding Walter Lee Irvin, who said at the time that McCall had committed deliberate murder. Late in 1955, Governor Collins and the Pardon Board unanimously commuted Irvin's death sentence to life imprisonment, despite the Parole Commission's recommendation that the death sentence be carried out. The action at the time was virtually unnoticed and unprotested.[11]

Two months later, after segregation had become an issue in the gubernatorial campaign, Lake County Circuit Court Judge Truman G. Futch ordered a grand jury investigation of the action of Collins and the Pardon Board. Futch based his order on receipt of three petitions signed by 121 citizens, mostly rural residents of Lake and Marion counties.[12] The grand jury invited Governor Collins and the Pardon Board to testify before it. The questioning of a governor's commutation of a death sentence was without precedent in Florida history. The *Tampa Tribune* speculated on such an extraordinary step by a judge well versed in the principle that the executive is not accountable to an investigating body for decisions within his discretionary authority. The timing of the long-delayed protest, the announcement that Sheriff McCall, political foe of Collins, was again a candidate running on a racist platform, and the contest in Lake County between Senator Ed Baker, a Pork Chopper, and a Collins supporter, Representative J. A. Boyd, were circumstances which the *Tribune* editorial writers considered more than coincidental. Collins thought so too, saying that there was "an implication of politics," but refusing to accuse anyone.[13] Collins justified his action in the Irvin case on the ground that many things were left undone and that the state didn't "walk that extra mile . . . did not establish the guilt of Walter Lee Irvin in an absolute and conclusive manner."[14] Collins declared that there was nothing to investigate "except LeRoy Collins' judgment and conscience—both beyond control or coercion of a grand jury. They are subject to review by God and the people of Flor-

11. *Tampa Morning Tribune*, editorial, February 24, 1956, sec. A, p. 16.
12. Jean Sneed, "Judge Calls Grand Jury Inquiry into Collins Part in Sparing Lake Rapist," *Tampa Morning Tribune*, February 17, 1956, p. 18.
13. *Tampa Sunday Tribune*, editorial, February 18, 1956, p. 4.
14. *Miami News*, February 16, 1956, sec. A, p. 10.

ida."[15] Collins did, however, offer to discuss the matter before newsmen with Judge Futch, the Lake County prosecutor, and the grand jury foreman at Tallahassee.

The temptation for segregationists to capitalize on this situation was too great. When Collins was about to ride in a parade at Eustis the following week, the rape victim confronted him with accusations. She was escorted by Sheriff McCall's deputies. Twenty-four hours earlier, the word had been out in Lake County that Collins' political enemies were planning such a confrontation in order to embarrass him. The rumor predicted that it would happen at a civic club dinner in Tavares, but the actual incident occurred the next morning at Eustis.[16]

The Irvin "issue" stayed alive. Judge Futch accused Collins of being "an innocent victim of the Communists by helping to save a Negro in the Groveland rape case from the electric chair."[17] The grand jury finally declared that Collins and the Pardon Board were legally justified in commuting the sentence, finding that both defense and prosecution were negligent in presenting the evidence. However, the grand jury charged that "false" statements and "lurid" newspaper stories influenced the commutation, specifically censuring Tom Harris, editor of the *St. Petersburg Times*, for a series of articles and the Reverend B. F. Wyland for circulating petitions for clemency.[18]

Collins was not permitted to forget the Groveland case during the campaign. Lowry criticized him in speeches, advertisements, and a pamphlet which he distributed. Later in the campaign, Peasley Streets, the otherwise inactive candidate, filmed an interview with the Groveland victim which was shown on television in Miami. The station immediately apologized for the showing, claiming that it didn't know the contents of the film. The other television channels in the state refused the film because it violated the standards of good taste and was unfit for showing in homes. Streets claimed, in a complaint to the Federal Communications Commission, that there was a conspiracy between Collins and the stations.[19] Fuller Warren also came to the defense of white womanhood. In an advertisement in the Broward edition of the *Miami Herald*, Warren

15. Ibid., February 17, 1956, sec. B, p. 9.
16. *Tampa Morning Tribune*, editorial, February 24, 1956, sec. A, p. 16.
17. *Miami Herald*, March 30, 1956, sec. A, p. 1.
18. *Florida Times Union*, May 5, 1956, p. 22.
19. Ibid.

asked, "Will LeRoy Collins ever explain to the citizens of Florida his shame and why he excused this Negro to the shame of every decent white woman of our state?"[20]

The second of these episodes involved the appointment by Collins of a black, Henry H. Arrington, as assistant State Attorney in Miami. The Arrington case was used in much the same way as the Groveland affair by the anti-Collins forces.

The black leadership in Miami had supported Collins in 1954 after the latter had promised to appoint some blacks to public office.[21] Collins made a few such appointments during his two-year term. Henry Arrington had been a trial attorney for the United States Department of Justice for four years before returning to Miami. Governor Collins appointed him, presumably upon recommendation of the black leadership to State Attorney George Brautigam, for Arrington stated that he never knew Collins or worked for him, and that he was acquainted with Brautigam only casually.[22]

Little notice was taken of the appointment before the gubernatorial campaign. However, on February 25, Arrington was invited to participate on a radio panel called "The People Speak." He was questioned regarding his work by the panel participants and by listeners who telephoned in questions. The program was tape-recorded by Ira David Hawthorne, organizer and president of the Dade County Property Owners Association, an ardent racist who had been questioned in the past by the federal grand jury which investigated bombings of black housing in Miami's Edison Center. In the recording, Arrington supposedly said that his work was not necessarily limited to cases involving blacks. Replying to questions regarding secretarial service, he quoted Brautigam as saying that secretaries who refused to take Arrington's dictation could "pick up their checks." The recording was immediately publicized. Arrington, who was in Washington at the time, was suspended by Collins pending investigation. State Attorney Brautigam denied flatly that his office was integrated, and he charged Arrington with "breach of confidence and misconduct" because

20. Advertisement by Fuller Warren, *Miami Herald*, Broward ed., April 29, 1956, p. 2.
21. Interview with Father Theodore Gibson, local NAACP president, March 17, 1964.
22. Interview with Henry H. Arrington, March 24, 1964.

his statements had stirred up the segregation issue.[23] Arrington returned, and claimed that the remarks were taken out of context. However, he made no attempt to defend his broadcast and, when Governor Collins dismissed him soon after, made no effort to fight dismissal.[24]

Six tapes of the broadcast were circulated throughout Florida, according to Hawthorne, who denied knowledge of how Lowry secured the tapes. He also denied supporting Lowry for governor.[25] However, Lowry used the tapes to good advantage, and lost no opportunity to comment on the affair in his speeches. In a broadcast in Miami, he spoke of Arrington as "the Washington lawyer sent to Florida in November 1954 to become a shining symbol of how integration is progressing in this state."[26] He went on to say that "Arrington chortles to the Communist-inspired NAACP that 'I have a white secretary and the office is fully integrated' despite the fact Collins claims there is no integration in Florida." Lowry asserted that discussion of Arrington's secretarial service or specific assignments was irrelevant. The placing of a black in an important executive position by Collins resulted in integration and provided a precedent for similar appointments.[27] As the tempo of the campaign progressed, Warren also charged Collins with starting integration by appointing Arrington.[28] Collins' prompt action in dismissing Arrington largely eliminated the incident from constant newspaper coverage. The tapes and speeches used by Lowry kept the episode alive, but its effectiveness as a campaign issue had been somewhat limited. Apparently neither Arrington nor the Miami black community blamed Collins for the dismissal, as their subsequent voting demonstrated. Arrington, speaking of it much later, expressed the belief that Collins had no alternative and that "it was a wise move for him to make at the time."[29]

The third of these incidents occurred shortly before the primary. As it was fresh in people's minds, it could be most effectively used by the segregationist forces. The African Methodist

23. *Miami Herald*, March 17, 1956, sec. C, p. 1.
24. Ibid., March 22, 1956, sec. A, p. 2.
25. *Miami News*, March 18, 1956, sec. A, p. 1.
26. Ibid., March 16, 1956, sec. A, p. 15.
27. *Florida Times Union*, March 20, 1956, p. 20.
28. *Miami Herald*, April 24, 1956, sec. A, p. 11.
29. Interview with Arrington.

Episcopal Quadrennial Convention was held at Dinner Key Auditorium in Miami, May 2–15. Thirty Miami Beach hotels had agreed to admit several thousand delegates and their families to the exclusion of their other guests.[30] This was the first time that large numbers of blacks were housed on Miami Beach, although some hotels had previously received delegates to predominantly white conventions.

For Collins, who claimed that Florida was segregated, the timing of the convention was most unfortunate. Lowry called it a "black day for the state of Florida" when blacks were being served by white waitresses at the hotels.[31] He made a telecast from Jacksonville on May 3 in which he showed films of delegates to the African Methodist Episcopal Convention eating in restaurants while white people were being served. He declared that such integration would be a great economic catastrophe for Florida.[32] Lowry charged in another speech that Collins could easily have ordered the sheriff to stop the race mixing, which was illegal, but that Collins refused to act because "he has sold out for the Negro block vote."[33] He claimed that the convention had so alarmed people in Dade County that he was making "terrific strides." He said that a door-to-door campaign for Lowry was fast gaining momentum.[34] Collins declared himself "shocked personally by that situation at Miami Beach." He said that he had not been consulted and, as governor, had no legal recourse to prevent it, for the Attorney-General's office had advised him that there was no law prohibiting a hotel or restaurant from serving guests whom it considers desirable. He suggested that neighboring property owners could get an injunction by claiming that a nuisance was created.[35]

The continuing problem of the Supreme Court order to admit Virgil Hawkins to the University of Florida Law School kept pace with those other incidents. All candidates agreed that this should be prevented; the disagreement was on methods of prevention.

30. *Miami Herald*, April 25, 1956, sec. D, p. 1.
31. *Florida Times Union*, May 3, 1956, p. 26.
32. Ibid., May 5, 1956, p. 18.
33. Ibid., May 3, 1956, p. 26.
34. *Miami Herald*, May 3, 1956, sec. A, p. 2.
35. John McDermott, "Candidates Doff Gloves for Final," *Miami Herald*, May 5, 1956, sec. A, p. 2.

Governor Collins called a conference of cabinet officers, legislative leaders, the Board of Control, the presidents of the state universities, and others concerned with education. After considerable advance publicity, they met in Tallahassee on March 21 to plan a fight against integration of the schools. Collins invited anyone with a plan to present it in writing to the conference. None of the candidates availed himself of the offer.[36] At the conference, Collins noted what he called "a dangerous deterioration in our racial relations," warning that the state could lose all the progress it had made in race relations unless reason prevailed. He proposed that President Eisenhower and Attorney-General Brownell call a conference of all the southern governors and attorney-generals to discuss the segregation problems of the South. The conference endorsed this suggestion and adopted four others: (1) that the conference formulate a resolution requesting the Supreme Court to reconsider the Hawkins case; (2) that if the hearing is granted, Collins accompany Ervin to plead the case for Florida; (3) that the Board of Education review the regulations set by the Board of Control regarding admission to the state universities; (4) that Collins and Ervin appoint a committee of legal experts to consider all proposals for retaining segregation and to present recommendations to the conference.[37] Collins declared that if the committee could propose legislation considered sound by legal authorities, he would then call a special session of the legislature. All participants at the conference pledged themselves to use every legal means to avoid integration in the schools. House Speaker Ted David declared at the close of the conference, "I think what we've done here today will definitely put us in the black."[38]

Collins, in his message to the President, stressed the sound and reasonable approach to the race problem taken by Florida, but he reminded Eisenhower that Florida was dedicated to maintaining the "tradition and customs of segregation, which are as deeply rooted in this state as in any other southern state."[39] He

36. John Boyles, "Candidates Ignore Collins' Offer," *Miami Herald*, March 25, 1956, sec. G, p. 2.

37. "Statement by Governor LeRoy Collins to Conference on Segregation, March 21, 1956," Misc. 1956, Collins Papers at University of South Florida Library, Tampa. See also *Miami Herald*, March 22, 1956, sec. A, p. 1.

38. Boyles, "Candidates Ignore."

39. *Miami Herald*, March 23, 1956, sec. C, p. 1.

warned that as a result of extremists on both sides, "we are experiencing a serious deterioration of racial relations." By offering to appear personally before the Supreme Court and by placing the segregation burden upon Eisenhower, Collins seized the initiative for a little while. As governor, he was in a position to act while his opponents could only make promises.

Lowry headquarters called the conference the "meeting of the integrationists."[40] Lowry promptly declared the conference to be a "whitewash." He said that Collins' request that Eisenhower call a conference of southern governors "is like hiring an attorney on the other side to plead your case. He may plead it but he won't win it."[41]

Bryant, at this point, felt called upon to offer more to the segregationists. Several days before Collins' conference met, he announced an eight-point program to combat integration. He proposed that a special session of the legislature be called to implement the results of the conference, that the legislature adopt an interposition resolution as a "protest," that appeals to the United States Supreme Court be left to the attorney-general, that the governor meet with his counterparts in the other southern states to create a united front, and that equal as well as separate school facilities be established rapidly.[42]

Fuller Warren took a more direct approach to the Hawkins case. He charged that Virgil Hawkins should be prohibited from entering the law school because he had brutally beaten two school children while he was a teacher in Lake County years ago. As proof, Warren released affidavits signed by four persons, including the principal of the school where the beatings were alleged to have occurred.[43] Hawkins denied the charge, and a number of Lake County school officials failed to recall such an incident. The Board of Control promised to investigate the charges.[44] Apparently they could not be substantiated, but the incident gave Warren considerable publicity as an active opponent of integration.

Lowry continued to hammer away on the efficacy of interposi-

40. *Florida Times Union*, March 17, 1956, p. 18.
41. *Miami Herald*, March 24, 1956, sec. B, p. 5.
42. Ibid., March 19, 1956, sec. C, p. 8.
43. Ibid., March 30, 1956, sec. A, p. 2.
44. Ibid., March 17, 1956, sec. C, p. 1.

tion. "Interposition will stop it cold," he said.[45] Interposition had never failed, according to Lowry. Collins responded that interposition was only a protest, and that the state had already protested the Supreme Court decree in a resolution adopted in 1955. He cited the experience of Virginia, which had adopted an interposition resolution and, despite this, had about 100 blacks in its state university while Florida had none.[46] Warren agreed with Collins that interposition was only a gesture. In his own fashion, he said, "some adult should tell the 'worthy warrior from Tampa' that interposition is just a high-sounding word which has no legal force since the North won the Civil War near [sic] ninety-one years ago." Talking of "this multimillionaire demagogue," Warren said he "ought to know that interposition cannot possibly succeed unless Florida seceded from the Union and won the resulting war against the United States."[47]

It must have been obvious both to Warren and Lowry that if Lowry picked up support on the segregation issue, it would have to come from those same rural areas that had previously backed Warren. Lowry attacked Warren for having entertained blacks at luncheon at the governor's mansion during his first term. Warren explained that a mixed group had visited his office in 1952 to protest the murder of a black at Mims. Having heard that they intended to demand service at a white restaurant and trying to avoid an incident, "I invited the delegation of White and Colored citizens, about fifteen in number, to go out to the mansion and eat some sandwiches."[48] "They entered the mansion through a side door, ate some sandwiches and left in about half an hour," he said.[49] Lowry had previously attacked Warren for an item veto of an appropriations bill which would have cut off funds from schools permitting integration. Lowry said, "Fuller Warren is the first governor of Florida to betray his oath of office and attempt to end segregation in our public schools and colleges. I can only warn the people of Florida to beware of this Judas kiss from the former governor."[50] The vetoed clause actually had no connection with the public schools, for it dealt with state col-

45. Delaney, "Interposition Will Stop It."
46. *Miami Herald*, April 7, 1956, sec. A, p. 4.
47. *Florida Times Union*, February 29, 1956, p. 21.
48. *Miami News*, March 19, 1956, sec. A, p. 17.
49. *Florida Times Union*, March 19, 1956, p. 20.
50. *Miami News*, February 22, 1956, sec. A, p. 7.

leges and universities. Warren had explained in his veto message that Florida's image in the nation would suffer, that the provision would violate teaching contracts and research agreements, and that he doubted its constitutionality.[51]

As Lowry continued the attack on him, and as he saw some support dwindling away, Warren shifted from his moderate position in a desperate effort to maintain his "Cracker" support. He made two proposals designed to save the state from integration.[52] The most important of these was a joint southern attempt to have the Fourteenth Amendment changed to permit each state to decide whether it wished to integrate. Second, Warren declared that he wouldn't wait for inauguration to attack the segregation problem. He would create a committee to help him immediately after the primary. Furthermore, Warren proposed to offer Lowry a position on this committee, conveniently forgetting that he had described Lowry as "the synthetic general," a "Johnny-come-lately who entered this segregation battle the lastest with the leastest."[53]

Lowry distributed a pamphlet accusing the other candidates of supporting integration. Collins' appointment of Arrington and his commutation of Irvin's death sentence were mentioned. Collins' membership in the United World Federalists was attacked and he was accused of having "caught the Moscow train shortly after World War II." Lowry's organization printed a picture of Collins shaking hands with a black. Collins explained that the picture was taken in Orlando at the meeting of the Florida Negro Teachers' Association, where he shook hands with the association officers when they welcomed him. "I cannot imagine any governor doing otherwise. Our Negro teachers have done and are doing a fine job for the state and I respect them for it."[54] Collins described the Lowry material as "filthy and scurrilous," declaring, "a man of character and integrity would not stoop so low."[55]

Lowry attacked Bryant for accepting integration. He said the *Tampa Daily Times* of January 21, 1956, had printed excerpts of a Bryant speech made to the Tampa Kiwanis Club on August 4,

51. Ibid., June 11, 1951, sec. B, p. 1.
52. Stephen Trumbull, "Is Collins Taking Off His Gloves?" *Miami Herald*, April 13, 1956, sec. B, p. 5.
53. *Miami News*, March 13, 1956, sec. A, p. 17.
54. Both quotes in *Florida Times Union*, April 25, 1956, p. 21.
55. *Miami Herald*, April 24, 1956, sec. A, p. 4.

1954, in which Bryant is alleged to have said of the Supreme Court decision, "the South has swallowed a lot of bitter pills in the past and has kept its head high. We've got to swallow it, we've got to be men enough, Christian enough, and Democrats enough to make the best of it."[56] Bryant said that his notes for the speech contained no such reference and that he never had the sentiments quoted.[57]

Lowry announced a program which would, in his words, "put the NAACP out of business." He would refuse to deal with them as governor and would order all state agencies to follow his example. He opposed the NAACP "for dragging Negroes to the polls to register," predicting that most of the Negro vote would be for Collins.[58] He promised that when he became governor, the Communists and the NAACP would never dominate or infiltrate the public schools, but he also said that he would provide equality of opportunity for all, regardless of race.[59] He declared that school integration meant only one thing—intermarriage.[60] In a speech at Lake City, Lowry announced another means of preventing integration. He explained that since the governor's signature is required by the Constitution on every check dispersing state money, "By refusing to sign checks to support mixed schools, I can guarantee that our schools will remain separate."[61]

By late March it had become apparent to experienced observers that Lowry had gained heavy support, especially in North Florida, at Warren's expense.[62] In the small counties enthusiastic listeners cheered his denunciations of integration. He talked of nothing except the segregation problem, but his listeners seemed equally absorbed in it. One reporter traveling with him said that only once during a whole day of whistle-stopping was Lowry queried on another subject. Lowry told of an incident in North Florida which clearly illustrated the interests of his Cracker audience. He said that he introduced himself to one potential voter as

56. *Florida Times Union*, May 3, 1956, p. 9.
57. Letter from Governor Farris Bryant to author, April 29, 1964.
58. Larry Birger, "Lowry Discounts Fuller as a Threat," *Miami News*, April 11, 1956, sec. A, p. 9.
59. *Florida Times Union*, April 19, 1956, p. 26.
60. *Miami News*, March 27, 1956, sec. B, p. 11.
61. *Miami Herald*, April 15, 1956, street ed., sec. B, p. 2.
62. John McDermott, "Estes Marks Gains While Fuller Falls," *Miami Herald*, April 8, 1956, sec. G, p. 3.

the candidate strongest for segregation. The man's reply was, "Yeah, that's okay, but what you going to do about those niggers?" Even Warren's supporters acknowledged the success of Lowry's appeal in the rural Panhandle. W. Turner Davis of Madison, president of the Senate and a Warren backer, predicted that Lowry would take the county. Senator S. D. Clarke, another Warren supporter, when questioned at Monticello, said, "if Fuller loses out, I'm for Sumter in the run-off."[63]

Collins recognized Lowry's growing strength. He warned voters that Lowry's approach would lead to violence. He promised, "we will have segregation in this state by lawful and peaceful means, and we will not have our state—our Florida which has such a bright future—torn asunder by rioting and disorder and violence and the sort of thing this man is seeking to incite."[64] Lowry in most of his speeches recommended maintaining segregation without violence. Nevertheless, he warned, "You'll have volence . . . if integration is attempted."[65] Jack Bell, *Miami Herald* columnist, wrote that Lowry, on a local television program, openly suggested that we "march on Washington and overthrow the Supreme Court, if necessary, to prevent integration."[66]

Collins continued to present the image of a racial moderate despite the Lowry attacks. He constantly proclaimed his allegiance to southern institutions and he lost no occasion to point to his record. Florida had remained segregated in its schools while some Deep South states had been forced to give way. However, it was in his presentation of the other issues that Collins sought to minimize the segregation factor as a threat to his re-election.

Warren's charge that Lowry had previously taken no part in the civil rights battle is particularly interesting when viewed in the light of Lowry's political preoccupations before 1956 and in subsequent years. Lowry before 1956 had led an American Legion attack on the United Nations, UNESCO, and the World Federalists. During the campaign, he continually referred to left-wing elements who were exploiting segregation "only as a sledge-hammer to attack the Constitution." He declared that his cam-

63. Jim Hardee, "Lowry Steals Warren Votes in Crackerland," *Orlando Sentinel*, March 28, 1956, n.p.
64. *Miami Herald*, April 28, 1956, street ed., sec. B, p. 1.
65. *Florida Times Union*, April 6, 1956, p. 20.
66. Jack Bell, "Election Results Give Us Reason to Cheer," *Miami Herald*, May 13, 1956, sec. G, p. 4.

paign was "a crusade to preserve the rights of the little children of Florida. I carry the flag for them."[67] As mentioned, he attacked Collins for his championship of internationalism as a state senator.

Although Lowry was named "Florida's Number 1 spokesman against integration" after the primary, his major interest appeared to be fighting communism, the United Nations, and federal encroachment on the Tenth Amendment. Eight policemen were required to remove him from a state Parents and Teachers Association council convention, where he denounced PTA interest in supporting the United Nations.[68] He proposed establishment of a new school to fight communism and teach patriotism at the University of Florida, offering to pay $12,000 himself for the first year's salary of a "proper" man to head the school.[69] He established his own organization, the Florida Coalition of Patriotic Societies, which distributed right-wing literature.[70]

In a letter of March 6, 1964, Lowry wrote, "To begin with, I entered the Democratic primary in 1956 for only one purpose— to alert the people of Florida to the fact that the 1954 Supreme Court decision on desegregation was the opening wedge of an effort to destroy the right of the people guaranteed by the 10th Amendment to govern and conduct their local affairs."[71] Is it possible that Lowry's interest in maintaining segregation was centered primarily on his dislike of federal encroachment, rather than his fear of integration?

67. *Florida Times Union*, March 23, 1956, p. 18.
68. Wilder, "General Sumter Lowry."
69. Louise Blanchard, "School for Patriots Proposed by Lowry," *Miami News*, December 12, 1958, sec. A, p. 6.
70. Wilder, "General Sumter Lowry."
71. Letter from General Sumter Lowry to author, March 6, 1964.

5. Economic Development and Other Issues

Wₕᵢₗₑ Sumter Lowry was busy convincing Floridians that he was the best man to fight integration, LeRoy Collins was selling himself as the best man for attracting industry to Florida and for maintaining the stable, progressive climate in which the economy would continue to grow. He was helped considerably by the continued prosperity and the bright prospects in the near future. But he was helped even more by a series of developments which, if coincidental, were hardly less than miraculous. If planned, then Collins achieved a public relations coup of gigantic dimensions. The first of these was the epidemic of feature articles on Florida in the national magazines. The second was the announcement, in the heat of the campaign, by multimillionaire industrialist Howard Hughes that he was bringing a huge aircraft industry to Florida as well as a $100 million medical center to Dade County.

The articles on Florida began in 1955 and continued throughout the campaign. By February, feature stories had appeared in *Fortune, Colliers, Saturday Evening Post, Kiplinger's Changing Times, Holiday, Look,* and *U.S. News and World Report.* All wrote of Florida's sound, stable government, favorable tax structure, and effective governor—Collins.[1] Many of the articles featured Collins on the cover. *U.S. News and World Report* ran a second article on Florida in April, with six pages of pictures and information on Florida's business, taxes, climate, and schools, including an interview with Collins. Segregation was not mentioned once.[2] The

1. John Bonner, "Is Publicity Too Much?" *Miami Herald,* February 22, 1956, sec. A, p. 21.
2. "Florida Gives Its Formula for Boom without a Bust," *U.S. News and World Report* 42 (April 13, 1956): 78–84.

Florida Development Commission, charged with promoting industry and tourism, declared on April 25 that Florida had received $831,040 worth of free publicity in radio and television time and in national publications in the first quarter of 1956.[3]

Collins' opponents suspected that the articles were planted. Bryant commented that Collins' national publicity was "peculiar."[4] Warren declared that Collins had secretly retained a "big time New York advertising agency with Los Angeles connections" to handle the publicity for his re-election. These, according to Warren, were hired through a Jacksonville advertising agency which was working for the state and openly handling Collins' publicity. The agency representatives revealed their hand, Warren asserted, when they supervised the release of the Howard Hughes announcement. When questioned, Robert Rowley, Miami representative of the New York firm Carl Byoir and Associates, said that he and William Utley of Los Angeles were Hughes' representatives, and that they were totally unconnected with the Collins campaign.[5] If Collins planned the publicity to coincide with his campaign, no one was able to prove it. Warren, when questioned years later about it, said that he thought that the stories were planted, but that he didn't know how or by whom.[6]

Warren accused Collins of taking credit for Florida's economic development, which, he declared, was a result of vigorous efforts made by the Warren administration. In a speech at Lakeland, he said, "I haven't seen smoke or payroll from these factories you have been hearing about." He labeled them "headline industries" and went on to talk of his own goal of having a minimum of one industry in every one of the sixty-seven counties.[7]

Late in February, Collins began his second annual midwestern tour to lure industry to Florida, accompanied by thirty business and industrial leaders from the state. He conferred with businessmen, spoke at businessmen's luncheons, and gave press conferences. A reporter on tour with Collins wrote from Cleveland, "The governor's sales talk virtually saturated this area by radio and

3. *Florida Times Union*, April 26, 1956, p. 24.
4. Ibid., April 19, 1956, p. 26.
5. John McDermott, "Warren Raps U.S. Publicity Given Florida," *Miami Herald*, April 18, 1956, street ed., sec. B, p. 1.
6. Interview with Fuller Warren.
7. *Florida Times Union*, April 1, 1956, p. 22.

television."[8] Favorable business comment followed in the Florida newspapers. George J. Leness, senior partner in Merrill, Lynch, Pierce, Fenner, and Beane, said, "Tours like this awaken latent interest and produce action." McGregor Smith of Florida Power and Light said that the tours would put dollars in the taxpayers' pockets.[9] Collins' sincerity and warmth left an excellent impression upon midwestern businessmen, who were duly quoted by Florida newsmen.

Industrialist Cyrus S. Eaton announced completed plans for the West Kentucky Coal Company, one of the largest in the world, to locate a $1 million loading and transfer dock at Port Tampa, along with an authorized purchase of $5 million in boats and barges. He said that Collins' tour had convinced his company that Florida had a bright industrial future, thus a need for coal.[10]

One of the most convincing arguments to those looking to the governor for strong industrial development was the announcement by Howard Hughes. These industries, according to Collins, would exceed Chemstrand (Florida's single largest industrial plant) in size and importance.[11] Del Webb, a Hughes associate, read the statement from Collins' office. He announced that the Dade County Commission had already been requested to set aside sixty acres of land near Jackson Memorial Hospital for the medical project, and that building space adjacent to the hospital had already been leased. The site of the aircraft plant was not disclosed, but Webb said that it would require thirty acres of space. "Mr. Hughes doesn't do things in a small way," he declared. The Hughes announcement credited Collins with persuading him to locate in Florida, saying that the governor "is just about the best salesman any state ever had."[12]

From time to time, reports were made on the progress of the project. Announcement was made when architects were engaged for the aircraft plant.[13] Collins indicated that he was in telephone contact with Hughes and that plans "are progressing nicely."[14]

8. Herbert Boyer, "Collins Mid-West Tour," *Florida Times Union*, February 28, 1956, p. 18.
9. Allen Morris, "Governor's Tours Are Paying Off," *Miami News*, March 9, 1956, sec. A, p. 8, home ed.
10. *Florida Times Union*, March 17, 1956, p. 18.
11. *Miami Herald*, April 10, 1956, sec. A, pp. 1–2.
12. Ibid., sec. A, p. 1.
13. Ibid., April 25, 1956, sec. A, p. 15.
14. *Florida Times Union*, May 6, 1956, p. 16.

Collins' three opponents naturally reacted unfavorably to the announcement, each in his own characteristic way. Bryant called it a "startling coincidence" that it came shortly before the primary, commenting also that no location for the aircraft project was announced.[15] Warren proclaimed it a "hoax," "designed to deceive and mislead the people of Florida into voting to give the present governor a second term"; Collins, when questioned regarding Warren's comment, said, "I don't want to damage the state by dignifying it."[16] Questioned eight years later, Warren declared that his recollections of the incident were somewhat vague, but that he recalls no proof that the proposed project was a hoax. "It must have been an instinctive reaction," Warren said regarding his comment.[17] Lowry's comment on the Hughes announcement was, "I cannot understand our governor's excitement over some man from out in California. This is the state, you know, where this Supreme Court Justice Warren came from—the man who said we have to put Negroes in white schools."[18]

There was no indication at the time that little of the Hughes projects would materialize. Actually, the medical research project was established in an office at Miami Beach. By 1961, it had received $24,900,000 from Hughes ($16,900,000 of which it returned to the Hughes Tool Company), with which it supported research in biochemistry, microbiology, and cardiovascular problems. Nothing was ever done about the aircraft company.[19] Collins' enemies still believe that the proposed aircraft plant was a hoax designed to get him votes. Newsmen for years amused themselves by asking Collins if he had heard from Hughes. He invariably laughed with some embarrassment and changed the subject.[20] Political writers John McDermott of the *Miami Herald* and Charles Hesser of the *Miami News* believe that the Hughes aircraft project was genuinely contemplated at the time.[21] One explanation offered is that Hughes ran into financial difficulties with stockholders of his various companies.

From a practical standpoint, the Hughes announcement was

15. Trumbull, "Is Collins Taking Off His Gloves?"
16. Both quoted in *Miami Herald*, April 12, 1956, sec. A, p. 17.
17. Interview with Fuller Warren.
18. *Miami Herald*, April 18, 1956, street ed., sec. A, p. 1.
19. Ibid., November 19, 1962, sec. A, p. 4.
20. Telephone interview with Charles Hesser, March 4, 1964.
21. Telephone interview with John McDermott, March 3, 1964.

the final proof Collins needed to demonstrate his effectiveness. He placed ads quoting Hughes' statement about his salesmanship. A Collins "victory tune" was written for his rallies:

> He made the legislature legislate
> He put roads in places that help the state
> He went travlin' North, met the V.I.P.s
> And he brought back millions in new industries
> Invested 16 bucks where we never got one
> He made folks like Florida's favorite son
> Floridians, here's a governor we must choose
> Or we'll lose that project with Howard Hughes.[22]

Along with the good salesman "pitch" went a corollary that industry would not move into an atmosphere of racial tensions and disorder where schools might be closed and the economy disrupted. Sylvia Porter, syndicated financial columnist, wrote that the Fantua Factory Locating Service, the largest plant locating consultants in the world, said that at least twenty corporations ready to move into the South were reconsidering because of the racial agitation. These projects alone involved jobs in the tens of thousands. She said that the racial problem had always been a factor, but that it had previously been offset by southern climate, lower wage levels, tax exemptions, and cheap power. Now these inducements could not lure industry in the face of impending disorder. Key employees were refusing to move into areas where schools were in jeopardy. Companies considering some states like North Carolina were frightened off by rising taxes in communities which had the cost of maintaining "separate but equal" schools.[23] Other articles appeared, quoting business leaders who said that racial unrest would affect business adversely.[24]

Lowry had his own economic interpretation. The South, he maintained, had lost millions in planned industry because of the Supreme Court decision. Industrialists had been moving South to avoid regimentation by Communists and other groups protected

22. John McDermott, "Gov. Collins Could Win in First Primary," *Miami Herald*, April 1, 1956, sec. G, p. 3.

23. Sylvia Porter, "Racial Tensions Scare Industry," *Miami Herald*, March 26, 1956, sec. A, p. 17.

24. Bert Collier, "Both Sides Use Boycott," *Miami Herald*, April 8, 1956, sec. A, p. 27.

by state civil rights codes. Now that the Court proposed to interfere in the South, the motive for moving industry was gone.[25]

While Warren and Bryant had presented business planks from the beginning, only insisting that they would provide better leadership in that regard than Collins, Lowry appears to have had second thoughts about his one-plank platform. He belatedly broadened his platform, promising to build more and better roads, to provide more modern school facilities, and to lure tourists and industry into Florida. Again he warned that if integration occurred, "it will create the greatest economic disaster in the history of Florida. You'll have misery and poverty. Your beaches and motels will be closed."[26] Lowry enumerated his business qualifications, spoke of his success in finance and in industry, and claimed that he would better understand business problems and that he had more experience than his "political lawyer" opponents.[27]

Few important issues other than segregation and industrial development arose during the campaign. Some controversy developed as to who deserved the credit or the blame for the Florida highways and over Warren's proposal for increasing homestead exemption. Argument continued over apportionment. Bryant discovered that Lowry was being supported by the Du Pont interests. And Collins, Bryant, and Lowry recalled Warren's record with disgust, while Warren himself pointed with pride to his administration.

Late in April, Bryant made a broadcast from Miami Beach in which he disclosed that Lowry was being supported by the Du Pont interests, accusing him of being Ed Ball's puppet. He revealed that Dan Crisp, a former Du Pont lobbyist and in 1956 still working for the St. Joe Paper Company, a Du Pont subsidiary, and E. H. Ramsey of Tampa, associated with Du Pont for years, were Lowry supporters.[28] Bryant went on to say, "The general may believe that segregation is the only issue in the campaign, but the Ed Ball–Du Pont interests who are providing the money for his lush campaign fund have their eyes elsewhere. Their real purpose is to keep the tax burden in Florida off the neck of the Du Pont interests and on the backs of the consumers."[29] Bryant said

25. *Tampa Morning Tribune*, March 17, 1956, p. 9.
26. *Florida Times Union*, April 4, 1956, p. 15.
27. Lowry campaign brochure, Lowry 1956, Collins Papers.
28. *Florida Times Union*, April 22, 1956, p. 17.
29. Ibid., April 28, 1956, p. 18.

that from personal conversations he had had with Ball, he knew that Du Pont sought to decrease the property tax burden on the hundreds of thousands of Du Pont acres by securing an across-the-board sales tax. The limited one effectuated in 1949 exempted food and drugs.[30]

Lowry then announced Ball's support with pride, saying he thought it was "a fine and healthy thing to see our distinguished citizens take an open stand like Mr. Ball." He and Ball were personal friends, he said, who agreed on the issues of segregation and states rights. Collins, when asked to comment, only said, "I thought that everyone had been knowing that all along."[31] Ed Ball said that he was backing Lowry personally, but that the Du Pont interests were not involved.[32]

While not of great moment in itself, the disclosure of Du Pont support could have done Lowry no service. It served to cast some suspicion upon his "crusade" for segregation. It may have alienated those who were acquainted with the Ball string-pulling in the past and who feared that an increased sales tax was Du Pont's primary objective in the election.

The campaign generated some disagreement over the Sixty-Seven Senator Amendment, to be voted on statewide the following November. Warren espoused it as part of his platform and Bryant endorsed it as well, both saying that it was the best plan yet proposed because it contained an automatic reapportionment process for avoiding future battles. The amendment would have granted each county one senator and would have made minor concessions in the House apportionment to the larger counties so that the population required to elect a majority of the Senate would have declined from 13 per cent to about 8 per cent, while the population required to elect a majority of the House would have increased from about 15 per cent to 27 per cent.[33] The sectional lines were very sharply drawn regarding this amendment, as can be seen from the vote in the November election: it was defeated 288,575 to 187,662, with almost all the larger counties against it. Warren justified the plan on the basis that there is a very real analogy between the federal government and the

30. Ibid., April 26, 1956, p. 24.
31. *Tallahassee Democrat*, April 22, 1956, n.p.
32. John McDermott, "It Looks Like LeRoy Collins Day in Florida Tuesday," *Miami Herald*, May 6, 1956, sec. G, p. 3.
33. Havard and Beth, *The Politics of Misrepresentation*, pp. 43, 53.

states, where each state has two senators regardless of size, and the state government and the counties.[34] Talking at Palatka, Warren blamed the big newspapers with absentee ownership for opposing the plan because they were bent on "squeezing every dollar out of the state possible."[35]

Governor Collins opposed the amendment, saying it would further the inequities of representation already existing. He called it "about the worst monstrosity to come down the legislative pike in years." He objected to the unreasonable size of the proposed legislature and predicted that if the amendment were adopted there would be discord between the two houses leading to stalemate and preventing constructive legislation. Collins also ridiculed the analogy between states and counties, saying that states are sovereign governments while counties are merely administrative units of states.[36]

Warren's proposal to double the homestead exemption drew fire from most quarters. Bryant said that it was "more like a sieve than a plank," warning that financial chaos would result.[37] Collins' supporters declared that the proposal "would close every school and bankrupt every town."[38] Fiscal experts warned that it would place an even greater burden on business property owners and that it would be necessary to require assessment at 100 per cent of present market values. Tax officials said that the $10,000 homestead exemption would be catastrophic. The $5,000 homestead exemption cost Dade County $19 million in 1956. The estimate was that a $10,000 exemption would cost an additional $10 million.[39] In Broward County, officials declared that they would "throw in the sponge" if the exemption were raised, because no city could survive such a revenue loss.[40] The Warren proposal did not fire the public imagination under such circumstances. Warren's own explanation of his proposal was that with costs of homes increasing, it was difficult to buy one under $10,000.[41] He anticipated 100 per cent assessment which would

34. Interview with Fuller Warren.
35. *Florida Times Union*, March 13, 1956, p. 19.
36. Ibid., February 21, 1956, p. 21.
37. *Miami Herald*, February 24, 1956, sec. A, p. 20.
38. Ibid., April 8, 1956, sec. A, p. 2.
39. C. C. Berning, "$5,000 Homestead Exemption Here to Stay," *Miami Herald*, April 15, 1956, sec. B, p. 1.
40. *Miami Herald*, April 1, 1956, Broward ed., p. 1.
41. Ibid., March 28, 1956, sec. C, p. 1.

have required nearly every homeowner to pay property taxes.[42] He said that the proposed exemption wouldn't have taken much revenue from the counties, because some assessed property for only 15 per cent anyway.

Highways were another point of contention, with candidates hurling charges and countercharges against each other. Warren, Bryant, and Collins all took credit for the Florida turnpike. However, since the turnpike was bob-tailed (cut short) by its opponents before 1955, when the legislature finally decided to build the whole road from Georgia to Miami, the waters were sufficiently muddied so that no clear-cut facts emerged. The *Miami Herald* entered the arena, charging that Warren didn't support the turnpike until late 1951, that former Senator Gautier was the individual most responsible for securing support for the turnpike in the legislature.[43] It criticized Bryant because, as speaker in 1953, he appointed legislators opposed to the turnpike as chairmen of the crucial Rules and Roads committees. Then, the *Herald* said, when public support for the turnpike could no longer be resisted, the compromise, bob-tailed turnpike was passed.[44] Bryant was furious, charging that the *Herald* misrepresented the facts. He said that actually he had led the fight for the pike and had saved it by promoting the compromise, and in 1955 he had worked to put through the full turnpike.[45]

Warren claimed that more roads were built during his administration than at any other time.[46] He made a series of appeals for votes in various localities by criticizing present or proposed construction which had some local opposition.[47] He made a special point of opposing the Collins administration's plans to build the turnpike west of Jacksonville, claiming that his administration had planned to have it feed into the Jacksonville Expressway. Warren's advertisements in the Jacksonville *Florida Times Union* promised the tie-in between the two highways if he were elected.[48] Warren also objected to the haste with which the Collins administration was validating the bonds for the turnpike.

42. Interview with Fuller Warren.
43. *Miami Herald,* April 9, 1956, sec. A, p. 2.
44. Ibid., March 28, 1956, sec. A, p. 6.
45. Ibid., March 27, 1956, sec. A, p. 10.
46. *Florida Times Union,* March 9, 1956, p. 21.
47. Ibid., March 31, 1956, p. 18.
48. Ibid., May 2, 1956, adv., p. 12.

He referred to the bill before Congress which proposed that the federal government provide 90 per cent of the cost of highways and the states only 10 per cent.[49] Warren insisted, even years later, that Collins had gotten a "mere fraction" of what Florida could have received from the federal government for highways.[50]

Collins spoke on television in Jacksonville defending the separation of the turnpike and the Jacksonville Expressway because it was in the best interests of the whole state. Furthermore, he said that it was neither sound business nor to the advantage of the people of Jacksonville to dump heavy traffic from the turnpike into the already difficult traffic situation in Jacksonville, citing engineering and financial studies which recommended the change.[51]

Bryant, in a bid for South Florida votes, charged that Collins had cut highway spending in Dade and Broward counties the previous year, using the diverted funds to build up his political fences in other areas.[52] Collins needed a heavy South Florida majority and he reacted promptly with an announcement several days later that the state would build a multimillion-dollar north-south freeway to relieve the heavily congested Dade County streets. State Road Board Chairman Wilbur Jones promised that the expressway would be started within a year.[53] Fuller Warren said that the promised expressway "appears to be another hoax cooked up to capture votes." Warren asserted that the expressway could be built only if the 1957 legislature were willing to appropriate funds and impose taxes to pay for it, saying that Collins was trying to "deceive the people of Dade County into thinking he's going to give them a great expressway project that hasn't been surveyed, that hasn't been planned, and that no money is on hand or has been provided for."[54] The State Road Board had the last word by pledging to build half the expressway with $2 million from the $8,535,000 tentatively earmarked for Dade primary road projects.[55] The promised expressway was con-

49. Ibid., March 28, 1956, p. 18.
50. Interview with Fuller Warren.
51. *Florida Times Union*, April 10, 1956, p. 30.
52. Ibid., April 18, 1956, p. 22.
53. *Miami Herald*, April 21, 1956, sec. A, p. 1.
54. Ibid., April 22, 1956, sec. B, p. 11.
55. James Miller, "State Pledges 2 Million for Miami Bypass," *Miami Herald*, April 24, 1956, sec. A, p. 2.

crete proof to Dade County residents that Collins intended to provide for their area.

Collins' office sent out information detailing the administration's activities not only in road-building but in all other areas, along with lists of 1955 expenditures, for use in public relations in each county by Collins' county headquarters.[56]

Fuller Warren's record as governor was an issue constantly disputed by the candidates. Warren defended his administration, listing its unquestioned accomplishments. However, he was vulnerable because of his refusal to appear before the Kefauver investigating committee and because of his signing the sales tax bill, despite his campaign pledge to veto it. Even before Warren announced his candidacy, Bryant declared, "If Warren does run, the principal issues will no longer be constitutional revision, economy, leadership, or even segregation, but the defense of our state against the locust horde of political henchmen, phonies, and cronies who wait in the shadows to feast upon the power and treasures of the people of Florida."[57] Collins opened his Miami campaign with an appeal to voters not to "turn back the clock to the days of greed and favoritism." He spoke immediately after Senator Gautier had reminded his audience that the Warren administration had "brought more discredit and more disgrace on Florida than anything in the history of our state."[58]

Warren challenged Collins to a debate on each man's public and private record. Collins' campaign manager said that Warren had reportedly been having poor turnouts and there was no advantage to Collins in helping Warren draw a crowd. Gautier, however, did offer to debate with Warren, and after Warren's repeated refusal to "let Collins' hatchet man do the dirty work on me,"[59] Warren finally did debate with Gautier in Miami. Gautier read the record of the Kefauver Committee linking racetrack owner Big Bill Johnson, the $100,000 contributor to Warren's 1948 campaign, with the Chicago underworld.[60] Warren retaliated with a whole list of insinuations against Collins. These charged

56. Memoranda from Collins' Tallahassee headquarters, Misc. 1956, Collins Papers.
57. *Miami News*, February 21, 1956, sec. C, p. 9.
58. John McDermott, "Collins Launches Campaign at Beach Tea and in Miami," *Miami Herald*, March 23, 1956, sec. A, p. 1.
59. *Miami Herald*, March 29, 1956, sec. A, p. 2.
60. Ibid., April 8, 1956, sec. A, p. 3.

Collins with accepting fees from a Miami racetrack and with making real estate deals on St. George Island for his personal profit while planning state improvements there.

Warren justified his refusal to appear before the committee by explaining that the federal government did not have the authority to subpoena a governor of a sovereign state. Much heat was generated on the subject of Warren's record. In another election, law enforcement might have been the key issue. In 1956, law enforcement as an issue was greatly overshadowed by the combination of desegregation, attracting industry, and the effect of the former upon the latter.

6. Campaign Techniques and Tactics

A RELEASE by the Associated Press on March 9 declared that the sound truck would be the major "vehicle of communication" between the gubernatorial candidates and the voters. Warren, Bryant, and Lowry announced plans to stump the state extensively. Only Collins, who had used the stumping technique to great advantage in 1954, said that he would concentrate his campaign on television, radio, and personal appearances.[1] Whistle-stopping was a skill in which Fuller Warren excelled. He was folksy, articulate, and always ready with an apt phrase or quip. He believed that talking to an unseen audience on television was "like kissing a pretty girl through a screen door."[2] It may be recalled that in 1956, Senator Estes Kefauver was receiving much publicity on his successful use of the person-to-person approach in his presidential primary campaigns.

In a discussion of Florida Panhandle politics, Herbert Cameron, *Florida Times Union* Tallahassee correspondent, wrote that people living in the area were serious about their politics and expected the old-fashioned fish fry and rally.[3] All the candidates used the handshaking and rally approach, giving fish fries, barbeques, and touring fairs, factories, and shopping centers.[4] Lowry's innovation in Florida campaign techniques was a drive-in rally in Jacksonville at the end of the municipal waterfront parking lot. Parking and mooring facilities were made available, and Lowry spoke from the deck of a boat moored alongside the parking lot.[5]

1. *Florida Times Union*, March 9, 1956, p. 21.
2. *Miami Herald*, April 9, 1956, sec. A, p. 1.
3. "Rally Keynote of Panhandle Politics," *Florida Times Union*, April 8, 1956, p. 21.
4. Lawrence Thompson, "Candidates Turning to Old Tried Ways," *Miami Herald*, April 15, 1956, sec. A, p. 15.
5. *Florida Times Union*, March 29, 1956, p. 21.

However, by April it had become obvious that political techniques were changing. The candidates, spurred on by Collins' television impact, were concentrating their efforts and their cash more and more on television and radio talks, foregoing the old fish-fry and hillbilly band technique to a considerable degree. Warren was the last holdout, adhering to the sound truck and handshaking methods more than the others.[6] Considering that a good deal of his support had been from the northwest area, this is not surprising. Warren and, to a lesser extent, Bryant made efforts to involve Collins in debate. Collins steadfastly refused, although he had used debate to his own advantage against Johns in 1954. As mentioned, he had good reason to believe that he could gain little from giving his opponents additional exposure.

Bryant, after resuming the campaign, tried to convert his financial disability into an advantage by attacking the "millionaire's race" of his competitors. He announced that he had refused offers of money from gambling and liquor interests. The wealthy, according to Bryant, wanted two dollars back for every dollar they contributed.[7] Therefore, he was waging a limited campaign with the support of the "little man."[8] It was in this vein that he attacked the Du Pont support of Lowry. It is interesting to note here that Bryant was not so concerned about a "millionaire's race" in 1960, for he received a total of $853,424 in contributions and spent $737,185 in order to get himself elected. He also solicited and accepted money from Ed Ball.[9]

Lowry, despite his financing by Ball, made a special bid for the workingman's vote by warning that the rich could escape integration but the poor would be unable to avoid it.[10] He made a sectional attack upon Warren in an effort to detach the latter's "friends and neighbors" vote in Northwest Florida, saying, "Warren was a West Florida boy, but when he got out of office, did he come back to live with you folks? No. He moved downstate to live with the rich people on Miami Beach."[11]

Warren recognized the impact Lowry had made upon his own

6. Ibid., April 7, 1956, p. 18.
7. *Miami News*, March 19, 1956, sec. A, p. 15.
8. *Miami Herald*, March 16, 1956, sec. A, p. 1.
9. Ibid., December 8, 1960, sec. A, p. 17. See also Robert Sherrill, *Gothic Politics in the Deep South* (New York: Grossman Publishers, 1968), p. 134.
10. *Florida Times Union*, March 9, 1956, p. 22.
11. McDermott, "Warren Raps U.S. Publicity Given Florida."

former adherents. He told his audiences "not to waste your vote on Sumter Lowry. Put me in the second race and I'll beat the present governor. I'm the only candidate that can beat him."[12]

The Warren newspaper advertisements were tailored for the area covered by the newspaper. His Dade County ads stressed the fact that he would be the first governor from Dade.[13] He insinuated that Collins was being financed by the Hialeah racetrack and that Collins' aides tried to suppress the Dade grand jury report, a major local issue at that moment.[14] In Jacksonville, Warren laid greatest emphasis upon segregation and upon the tie-in between the Florida turnpike and the Jacksonville Expressway.[15]

Collins likewise endeavored to prove his concern with local problems. In one Jacksonville ad, he showed a map of the roads and bridges, outlining recent construction with the caption "Here's What Gov. LeRoy Collins' Administration Has Done for Duval's Roads and Bridges."[16] He emphasized what he had done and could do for business, and his record of clean government and progress statewide. In a *Miami Herald* ad, he quoted Howard Hughes, Ralph McGill, and *Time* and *Look* articles which lauded his administration.[17]

The Lowry ads were in line with his one-plank program. Only at the very end of the campaign did he begin to sell himself as a businessman as well. Bryant, hampered by a shortage of funds, hardly advertised at all.

The *Atlanta Constitution*, writing of the Florida primary, called it a "heated contest, filled with an amount of sound, fury, and recriminations quite unnatural for the usually sensible citrus state."[18] The 1956 campaign was certainly distinguished by a greater amount of name-calling than usual. Warren, under personal attack, and adept at phrase-making, led the field. He called Bryant "the Ocala character assassin with the Harvard accent" and the "frenzied little office seeker" after Bryant had called his platform "diabolical, demagogic, and dangerous."[19] Warren termed

12. *Miami Herald*, April 28, 1956, st. ed., sec. B, p. 1.
13. *Miami News*, March 17, 1956, sec. A, p. 2.
14. *Miami Herald*, May 1, 1956, sec. D, p. 7, and May 3, 1956, sec. D, p. 7.
15. *Florida Times Union*, May 2, 1956, p. 12.
16. Ibid., May 4, 1956, p. 25.
17. *Miami Herald*, April 28, 1956, sec. A, p. 10.
18. As quoted ibid., May 7, 1956, sec. E, p. 3.
19. *Miami News*, March 12, 1956, sec. A, p. 10.

Lowry "a one-star political general firing verbal blanks,"[20] and "that millionaire ex-general who scooped up a fortune in a lucky insurance operation." A Warren flyer referred to Collins as the "curley-haired boy up in Tallahassee—the friend of the N-double-A-Cee-P."[21]

Lowry called his opponents "political lawyers" who were supported by entrenched political machines.[22] He ridiculed Collins' "mouthings" about promoting industry, saying that Collins "scarcely knows which end of the smokestack the smoke comes from."[23] Lowry called Warren "this warmed-over comedian."[24] One of Lowry's pamphlets represented all his opponents as integrationists and tools of the NAACP and enraged them all. Collins was particularly outraged because of the declaration that he had "caught the Moscow train." He referred to the "smear" in a speech at Tampa, saying, "No man of honor and integrity would use a pamphlet of that kind no matter how desperate he became."[25] He spoke of Lowry as a "one-track" candidate embarked on a course of inciting hatred and disorder. Referring to Warren, he spoke of "buffoonery and demagoguery."[26] Bryant was not to be outdone. He called Lowry a "puppet for Ed Ball and the Du Pont interests."[27] He spoke of Collins' "lame" administration and of Warren's "shame" administration.[28]

20. *Miami Herald*, February 27, 1956, sec. B, p. 1.
21. As quoted in J. E. Dovell and D. G. Temple, "Florida's Democratic Gubernatorial Primary for 1956," *Florida's Business* (January–March 1957): 19.
22. McDermott, "Three Candidates Look Alike."
23. *Florida Times Union*, April 13, 1956, p. 22.
24. Ibid., February 29, 1956, p. 21.
25. *Miami News*, April 26, 1956, sec. D, p. 5.
26. *Florida Times Union*, April 25, 1956, p. 21.
27. Ibid., April 28, 1956, p. 18.
28. *Miami News*, March 11, 1956, sec. A, p. 4.

7. Sources of Support

THE DISCLOSURES of the Kefauver Committee about the advance underwriting of Warren's 1948 campaign by three millionaires, as well as the exceedingly expensive Pepper-Smathers race in 1950, spurred passage of a campaign expense law.[1] A $1,000 ceiling was placed on total individual contributions, and candidates were required to file with the Secretary of State each week a record of their collections, names of contributors, and itemized expenditures. No contributions could be made by corporations, by persons with racetrack permits or liquor licenses, or by officers or directors of public utilities franchised by the state. No restriction was placed on the total expenditure in a campaign, however.[2] The 1955 legislature made further changes in an effort to reduce campaign expenditures. It moved the qualifying date up to February 21–March 6, hoping that by shortening the campaign period, less would be spent. It also forbade any campaign spending before February 21 except for personal travel.[3] For the 1954 primary, the candidates began campaigning in October 1953. Johns, Odham, and Collins together spent over $600,000 for the first primary.[4]

Despite the four months or so cut from the campaigning time, the four major candidates in 1956 spent $650,000: Collins spent $291,183, Lowry $115,216, Bryant $63,048, and Warren $194,682.[5] The cost of television time was so high and the use of that media so important in modern campaigning that despite the excellent intentions of the new law, campaign expenditures remained as high as ever. In the four primaries between 1952 and 1956, the

1. Price, *The Negro and Southern Politics*, pp. 122–23.
2. Havard and Beth, *The Politics of Misrepresentation*, p. 85.
3. *Florida Times Union*, April 22, 1956, p. 25.
4. *Miami Herald*, April 23, 1956, sec. B, p. 1.
5. Price, p. 97.

candidate spending the most money received the most votes.[6] Collins' advantage in this respect was certainly great, and Bryant's disadvantage in having about one-fifth the funds available to Collins was equally plain.

The sources of campaign contributions were not as apparent as would first appear. It was difficult to prove that contributions were actually given by individuals in greater amounts than permitted by law and attributed to a number of other persons, but it was nevertheless obvious that this was probably happening.

Collins was in a more favorable position to obtain endorsements and campaign workers as well as financial backing. Often the incumbent has a ready-made organization while the others have to build from almost nothing. In Collins' case, however, his major disadvantage was that he had appointed many of his former campaign workers to public office. Public employees in Florida were prohibited from campaigning. While Collins had the nucleus of an organization, most of his key people were unavailable to him. For example, the 1954 chairmen of his Hillsborough, Volusia, Suwanee, Lee, Orange, Pinellas, and Dade county organizations were either serving on the state Supreme Court, the Circuit Court, or the various state boards and commissions.[7]

Information on campaign organization and supporters has been rather inconclusive, but it has been possible to glean some facts. In vote-rich Dade County, Collins had the active backing of Senator R. B. (Bunn) Gautier and former Representative William C. Lantaff. Gautier kept up a constant running battle with Warren, attacking Warren's record with a vehemence which Collins might have considered unbecoming for himself.[8] Colonel Jack A. Younger resigned as president of the Dade County Crime Commission, a private organization devoted to fighting racketeering, to work for Collins. He declared that he was apprehensive that big-time racketeering would return to Florida if Warren were elected again.[9] In populous Broward County, incumbent Speaker of the House Ted David sacrificed running for re-election to give his time to Collins' campaign.[10] Probably the most important of his supporters, though, was Brailey Odham, whose

6. See illustration no. 1 in Appendix.
7. *Miami Herald*, February 13, 1956, sec. A, p. 23.
8. *Miami News*, March 23, 1956, sec. A, pp. 1, 10.
9. *Miami Herald*, April 4, 1956, sec. A, p. 1.
10. *Florida Times Union*, March 6, 1956, p. 18.

ability to hold a statewide following and to transfer its votes to another candidate was regarded with awe by many observers.[11] Odham, under pressure from Warren, resigned from the Inter-American Trade and Cultural Center Authority to campaign for Collins, saying that he would "walk through Florida barefooted" to prevent Warren's election.[12]

Although Bryant had been preparing for the campaign for three years, he had such difficulty obtaining support that shortly after he announced his candidacy, he declared that he might withdraw from the campaign because he couldn't raise the necessary money. Several days later he announced that supporters had come through with enough funds for him to conduct a limited statewide race.[13] Bryant's support was largely concentrated in Marion County with state Senator L. K. Edwards and Representative William Chappell behind him. His state chairman was James Kynes, at that time an Ocala attorney. Bryant had no organization at all in some counties.[14]

Warren entered the campaign with part of his old organization intact. He had considerable support in North Florida, including many influential state legislators. His campaign contributions were statewide, with much money coming from Dade County.

Lowry, on the other hand, had to build an organization from nothing, and many North Floridians who would have been his logical supporters were already committed to Warren. According to his own testimony, he had no pledged financial assistance.[15] Despite this initial disadvantage, he made tremendous progress throughout the campaign. His public relations advisor was Dan Crisp of Jacksonville, who had been a Du Pont lobbyist for many years and had worked for Senator Smathers in his successful campaign against Senator Pepper in 1950.[16]

Lowry's state campaign manager, Joe Jenkins, was a former commander of the Florida American Legion. Although Lowry had not previously run for office, he was by no means unknown or

11. Tom Raker, "Odham Helps to Sell Cabinet $50,000 Job," *Tampa Morning Tribune*, January 29, 1956, sec. A, p. 25.

12. *Miami Herald*, April 22, 1956, sec. A, p. 26.

13. Ibid., March 16, 1956, sec. A, p. 23.

14. *Tampa Sunday Tribune*, March 11, 1956, p. 16. See also letters to Collins from his campaign workers, 1956 Collins Papers.

15. Lowry letter.

16. John L. Boyles, "No One Wants a Special Session." *Miami Herald*, March 18, 1956, sec. G, p. 2.

without political connection; he had been regional director for the 1952 Eisenhower drive in Florida and had long-time National Guard and American Legion contacts. Lowry says that his "principal supporter" was Ed Ball of Du Pont but that, in general, he had little business backing.[17] Knowledgeable observers believed that he had ample campaign funds, despite a television appeal for money for his "crusade."[18]

Traditionally, candidates, especially incumbents, had been able to count on the active support of state employees. Under a new state law, career state employees were prohibited from active campaigning and from taking a leave of absence to campaign for a candidate.[19] The law was designed to protect career employees from political pressure, and in 1956 it was successful in operation. Tallahassee had one of the quietest campaigns observers could remember, while state employees were required to abstain even from placing bumper strips on their cars. One practical effect of this law was to remove an advantage which Collins would probably have enjoyed.

Organized labor took no official position in the gubernatorial primary. The AFL–CIO political arm, COPE, printed a list of endorsed candidates in the May 8 primary, but it failed to endorse a gubernatorial candidate, although it was believed that a majority of state labor leaders preferred Collins. Collins, Warren, and Bryant each claimed that he was supported by the rank and file of organized labor, of whom there were over 150,000.[20] There is little evidence that labor voted as a unit for anyone.

While conclusive proof of Collins' business support throughout the state is not available, widespread newspaper support and heavy contributions indicate that Collins was the choice of businessmen, particularly in peninsular Florida. The contribution lists from Dade County clearly show that Dade business was behind Collins. Among his contributors were Arthur Vining Davis, multimillionaire South Florida investor, William D. Singer, then owner of the Royal Castle hamburger chain, Roy Hawkins of the huge Florida Bessemer Properties, Frank Rooney, the largest general

17. Lowry letter.
18. Boyles, "Special Session."
19. Herbert Cameron, "Merit Plan No-Politics Rule Effective," *Florida Times Union*, April 1, 1956, p. 22.
20. Bryan Donaldson, "State Labor Heads Leaning to Collins," *Miami Herald*, April 15, 1956, sec. B, p. 5.

contractor in Florida, J. A. Cantor, millionaire real estate developer, Ben Novack, owner of the Fontainebleau Hotel, and a number of officials of the Keyes Company, largest real estate company in the South. Collins' banking support included Lowry Wall, chairman of the board of the Miami Beach First National Bank, Paul Scott, attorney for the First National Bank of Miami (and for the Florida Power and Light Company), Jack Gordon, president of the Washington Federal Savings and Loan Association, George B. Caster of the Coral Gables Savings and Loan Association, and Shepard Broad of the American Savings and Loan Association.[21]

Negro leadership lined up behind Collins in 1956. Its importance can be assessed from the black Democratic registration, which had risen to an all-time high of 128,437. A solid black vote for a major gubernatorial candidate was of great importance in placing him in the run-off or in giving him a majority.[22] It was generally agreed by all the candidates that the black vote would be significant. Bryant, Warren, and Lowry all declared that the black didn't want integration. Collins was conveniently unavailable for comment.[23]

Solicitation of the black vote has at times backfired on a candidate. One of the factors in the Smathers defeat of Pepper in 1950 was the publicizing of the pro-Pepper CIO–PAC registration drive among blacks, despite Pepper's efforts to dissociate himself from it.[24] Candidates have generally solicited the black vote while reassuring whites that they are not pro-Negro. Usually they met privately with black leaders, giving them such assurances as they could.

Most information on Collins' relationship with a black community was from Miami, but judging from the vote in the other large centers of urban black population, it is not unreasonable to assume that their situations were similar. Collins, using considerable discretion, continued to solicit the black vote, despite the difficult racial situation into which Lowry had maneuvered him. The Dade County Young Democratic Alliance was composed of the most prominent of the Miami black leaders, including as

21. *Miami Herald*, March 27, 1956, sec. A, p. 19; April 3, 1956, sec. A, p. 14; April 24, 1956, sec. A, p. 10.
22. Price, p. 97.
23. Ron Levitt, "Negro Vote Will Carry Weight," *Miami Herald*, April 16, 1956, sec. A, p. 26.
24. Price, pp. 60–63.

its second vice-president the Reverend Theodore Gibson, local NAACP president. Collins met with them, obtained their endorsement as he had in 1954, and even attended a public rally at the Mount Zion Baptist Church. Warren also solicited black votes in Miami, meeting with black teachers at the Dr. Phar Funeral Home. Bryant made no real effort to solicit the black vote, at least in Miami, and was considered an unknown quantity by the Negro leadership in 1956.[25]

The problem of the Dade County Young Democratic Alliance was to raise the registration figures, which were comparatively low in proportion to population. Some 35,000 to 40,000 persons were eligible to vote, but registration was less than half that figure. Black leaders made a concentrated drive for black registration.[26]

In Miami, the Alliance held rallies, made speeches, distributed flyers and small endorsement cards, and paid for large advertisements in the *Miami Times*, the local black weekly.[27] The latter did not endorse Collins. Its owner and former editor, H. E. S. Reeves, explained that although the paper was solidly behind Collins, "We did not want to hurt him."[28] Reeves said that the racial climate at that time, even in Miami, was such that his paper believed endorsement of a candidate would be used to that candidate's disadvantage in the white community. In 1956, the *Miami Times* contented itself with writing, "Let us look at the record of the candidates. You have heard them on television and you must have read or heard quite a lot about some of the methods some candidates are using to secure votes in this campaign."[29]

Actually, black registration rose from 119,000 in 1954 to 128,000 in 1956. Although it was lower in Dade and Duval than it had been in 1954, in areas like Tampa it rose to its highest level. However, the importance of black support can be readily seen from the voting figures, for they voted as much as ten to one for Collins.[30]

25. Interview with Father Gibson.
26. *Miami Times*, February 4, 1956, p. 1.
27. Telephone interview with Lloma G. Green, 1956 Executive Secretary of Dade County Young Democratic Alliance, February 25, 1964.
28. Interview with Reeves, February 27, 1964.
29. *Miami Times*, editorial, April 28, 1956, p. 4. Several years later, the *Miami Times* began endorsing candidates.
30. Price, pp. 57–58, 65.

ROLE OF THE PRESS

Collins received the support of all but one of the Florida daily newspapers which made an endorsement. In a survey of forty Florida dailies, twenty-one endorsed Collins, one endorsed Bryant, and the remainder took no stand. Bryant's hometown paper, the *Ocala Star-Banner*, was his sole supporter. The *Miami Herald, Tampa Tribune, St. Petersburg Times, Orlando Sentinel, Miami News, Tallahassee Democrat, Bradenton Herald, Fort Pierce News-Tribune, Fort Myers News-Press, Sarasota News, Fort Lauderdale Daily News, Lakeland Ledger, Winter Haven News Chief, Palatka Daily News, Sanford Herald, Lake Wales Daily Highlander,* and *Miami Beach Sun* were among Collins' backers. The influential *Florida Times Union* of Jacksonville remained neutral, but nearly all the other large city newspapers were behind Collins. He received support even in the Florida Panhandle, as was reflected by the endorsement of him by weeklies in Port St. Joe, Chattahoochee, Chipley, and Havana.[31]

Among the editorial comments favoring Collins, the *Winter Haven News Chief* wrote, "Collins is the Best," commenting that neither Warren nor Lowry could do the outstanding job done by Collins in selling Florida.[32] A *Miami News* editorial said, "Today there is little of literate America that does not recognize the name of LeRoy Collins, governor of Florida. That is not the slick promotion of a politician. That is the sound and statesmanlike leadership of a good governor. Under Governor Collins, Florida has achieved such a standard of integrity, stability, and progress as never before in its history."[33] The *Miami Herald* referred to the esteem accorded Collins and to the new climate of integrity and efficiency in the executive branch.[34] The *Daytona Beach Morning Journal* took the position that the racial agitation "carries a built-in threat to the economic development of the South."[35] On the dangers of extremism, the *Tampa Tribune* wrote, "As a matter of cold practicality, then, what sense does it make for Florida to abandon its present favored position to indulge in an emotional spree and suffer the inevitable hangover? . . . In these troubled

31. *Miami Herald*, April 22, 1956, sec. G, p. 3.
32. As quoted in *Tampa Sunday Tribune*, March 18, 1956, sec. A, p. 33.
33. *Miami News*, editorial, May 6, 1956, sec. C, p. 2.
34. *Miami Herald*, editorial, March 24, 1956, sec. A, p. 6.
35. As quoted in *Miami News*, March 25, 1956, sec. D, p. 11.

times, Florida is fortunate to have a governor who shuns the low road of demagoguery for the high road of statesmanship."[36]

The newspapers were not content only to endorse Collins: they attacked his rivals with vigor. The *Tampa Tribune*, which renewed a feud from Warren administration days, blistered the "Same Old Fuller Warren," referring to his "demagogic appeals" and to his campaign pledges which promised something for everyone. His program, the *Tribune* declared, was "carefully calculated to influence the unthinking, to-heck-with-the-other-guy, what's-in-it for-me type of citizen."[37] The papers repeatedly referred to the Warren record, emphasizing the Kefauver refusal, the multimillionaire backers, and the scandals. Warren reacted with vehemence, attacking "wealthy Yankee" absentee ownership of papers like the *Tallahassee Democrat* and the *Tampa Tribune*.[38] He took a quarter-page ad in the *Tribune* to object to an unsubstantiated charge made against him, saying, "From past experience, I have come to expect low blows from the absentee owned *Tampa Tribune*."[39]

Lowry fared as badly as Warren. Editorials blasted the injection of the race issue and the one-plank platform, emphasizing the dangers of stirring up hatred and violence. The *Tallahassee Democrat* said it was "disturbing to find a candidate entering the contest with no other apparent plank in his platform—no mention of the other vital affairs of government." The *Fort Myers News-Press* said of Lowry's candidacy, "It is deplorable indeed to find a candidate seriously seeking the governorship in the year 1956 on a platform of racialism. It will be even more deplorable if the other candidates continue to dignify the 'issue' by debating with him." Warning of the danger of Lowry's candidacy, the *Tampa Tribune* wrote, "It's no trick to play catch with a hand grenade and the stunt may impress the grandstand. The trouble is, a lot of innocent people can get hurt."[40] The *St. Petersburg Times* said that Ed Ball's backing of Lowry indicated that the segregation issue, "the one-tune repertoire of the soldier from Tampa," was being exploited for "economic political purposes. It raises the

---

36. As quoted ibid., February 12, 1956, sec. A, p. 19.
37. *Tampa Morning Tribune*, editorial, February 23, 1956, p. 16.
38. *Florida Times Union*, March 10, 1956, p. 18.
39. *Tampa Sunday Tribune*, March 11, 1956, sec. A, p. 28.
40. All quoted in *Miami News*, February 12, 1956, sec. A, p. 19.

question of who would be the governor if Lowry were elected—
Lowry or Mr. Ball?"[41]

A number of the newspapers commented favorably on Bryant,
even while endorsing Collins. The *Winter Haven News-Chief*
said, "Right now we feel that Bryant isn't the man for the present term." Some newspapers seemed to believe that he was only
warming up for the 1960 contest. The *Ocala Star-Banner* considered his unusual talents and abilities and endorsed his candidacy, but the *Miami Herald* found him unimpressive, commenting on his responsibility for the two-year delay in construction
of the full state turnpike.[42]

Lowry and Bryant each made separate statements complaining
about the favored treatment that Collins was given by the press.
Each accused the Miami papers of instituting a news blackout on
them. Bryant said, "They have a candidate but they're blanking
out other candidates. They're making misstatements of facts and
I resent their efforts to misrepresent me in the race for governor."[43] Bryant later said, "The only way I can get my name in the
Miami Herald is to say something blasting the Herald."[44] It may
be noted that Bryant made the same claim during his 1960
campaign.[45]

Lowry claimed that the press was so hostile that he was reluc-
tant to grant interviews.[46] The Lowry forces were apparently
quite upset over their treatment by the Miami news media,
judging from an incident which occurred at WTVJ–TV, Miami.
The candidate and his campaign manager, Joe Jenkins, arrived at
the studio to make a fifteen-minute paid political talk. Finding
that arrangements like backdrops, notestands, and the like had
not been prepared, Lowry grumbled but Jenkins was so enraged
that he spat tobacco juice across the studio floor. He continued
to spit on the floor saying, "That's what I think of you and
your ——— station," despite repeated requests that he stop.[47]
Some Lowry backers wanted to keep the incident from leaking

41. Quoted in *Miami News*, May 6, 1956, sec. A, p. 9.
42. All of these quoted in the *Tampa Morning Tribune*, January 22, 1956,
sec. A, p. 27.
43. *Florida Times Union*, April 22, 1956, p. 23.
44. Ibid., April 26, 1956, p. 24.
45. Interview with Hesser.
46. Delaney, " 'Interposition Will Stop It.' "
47. *Tallahassee Democrat*, April 24, 1956.

out if they could, but Lowry said, "Oh, don't worry about it. It'll help us in West Florida."[48]

There is no doubt that Lowry did not receive the news coverage in Dade that he received in the *Florida Times Union*, for instance. Several explanations have been offered for the alleged "blackout." *Miami Herald* political writer John McDermott wrote that Lowry repeated himself and that that is the reason he didn't receive the news coverage he expected.[49] Also denying a news blackout on Lowry, *Miami News* editor Bill Baggs, a columnist in 1956, said that Lowry was actually good copy, but that he tended to avoid Dade County in his campaigning. Baggs' explanation was that Lowry must have concentrated his activities elsewhere because a good part of the Gulf Life Insurance Company clientele in Florida was composed of Dade Negro citizens who might retaliate against the company, knowing Lowry's connection with it.[50] Actually, Lowry was forced to resign from the board of Gulf Life the day after he announced his candidacy because the company was threatened with a boycott.[51] As an important stockholder, his relationship with the company might have occasioned actual boycott if Negro leaders had considered him a real threat to Collins.[52]

In trying to assess the influence of the press in the primary, several factors must be considered. First, there was scarcely a town in Florida where the daily newspapers were not sold, usually on the day they were published. This was particularly true of the metropolitan papers like the *Miami Herald*, which published a Broward, Palm Beach, Brevard, and state edition, the *St. Petersburg Times*, the *Tampa Tribune*, the *Orlando Sentinel*, and the *Florida Times Union*.[53] Second, the newspapers tended to represent the attitudes of the urban areas. All but the *St. Petersburg Times* were conservative in outlook, usually reflecting the Chamber of Commerce position about government. The unanimity of support for Collins must have been rather decisive in influencing the voters. Certainly Collins' adversaries thought so.

48. Wilder, "Gen. Sumter Lowry."
49. John McDermott, "Collins May Win Upset in Jacksonville," *Miami Herald*, April 29, 1956, sec. G, p. 3.
50. Interview with Bill Baggs, editor of the *Miami News*, March 11, 1964.
51. *Florida Times Union*, April 1, 1956, p. 22.
52. Interview with Father Gibson.
53. Havard and Beth, pp. 228–29.

Lowry wrote, "The Miami papers certainly had a great influence on my defeat as a large part of the vote was in Dade County, served by its papers."[54] Warren, when questioned on the subject, said that the newspapers were "pretty fair" in factual coverage, but that their backing of Collins was "overwhelmingly important" to the outcome of the contest.[55]

54. Lowry letter.
55. Interview with Fuller Warren.

8. Effects of the Primary

W<small>HILE THE</small> gubernatorial campaign was taking place in Florida, much was happening elsewhere. The impending crisis between Israel and Egypt, the Khrushchev denunciation of Stalin, the Soviet dissolution of the Cominform, and the continuing rebellion in Cyprus dominated the international news. National attention was held by Eisenhower's decision to seek a second term, speculation over the possible "dumping" of Nixon, Senator Case's disclosure of a bribe offer by the natural gas lobby, Eisenhower's subsequent veto of the natural gas bill, and the Stevenson-Kefauver rivalry in the presidential primaries. But none of these events, regardless of its importance, was given the television, newspaper, and periodical coverage devoted to the courtship and marriage of actress Grace Kelly and Prince Rainier of Monaco.

A number of events in Florida, only remotely related to the campaign, usurped the headlines. The President-designate of the Senate, Harry King, was tried on a bribery charge connected with his campaign for re-election. Stevenson and Kefauver stumped Florida competing for presidential primary votes, and the State Attorney in Dade County attempted to suppress a grand jury report rebuking two Circuit Court judges for looting the estate of an elderly couple. The grand jury revelations occupied almost totally the front pages of the Dade County newspapers in the days just preceding the primary.

A final statewide poll by the Florida Political Survey Poll, conducted by Joe Abrams and released April 29, a week preceding the primary, gave Collins 43 per cent of the vote, Warren 23 per cent, Lowry 20 per cent, and Bryant 13 per cent. Nevertheless, it recognized Lowry's growing strength, noting, "His campaign is hot and he could be very dangerous by election time."[1] A telephone poll conducted in Dade County April 22–25 by University of Miami Professor Ross Beiler, ordered by Collins' Dade headquarters, revealed that Collins led in Dade with 78.5 per cent of the vote.[2] A Dade County victory of such proportions would have given Collins the possibility of a first primary victory if his support in other areas did not fade.

A Collins victory was generally expected by most major political reporters. However, an *Orlando Sentinel* round-up of predictions throughout the state revealed that only John McDermott of the *Miami Herald* anticipated that Collins would win in the first primary.[3] McDermott based his forecast partly on the reports that Warren might not carry Duval County. He believed that unless Warren won Duval handily, Collins could win a majority.[4] McDermott also used as basis for his prediction the 1952 primary, where McCarty barely missed winning in the first primary by 2,500 votes. He believed that Collins was better known than McCarty had been. Lowry was reported as early as April 15 to have pulled ahead of Warren into second place. Bryant was figured to finish last.[5]

Out-of-state interest in the Florida primary was high. The *New York Times* reported on the impending contest, writing that the major issue was segregation and the chief target Collins.[6] The *Atlanta Constitution* speculated on whether Florida would follow Collins' progressive leadership or "be led up the blind alley of hate and prejudice."[7] Drew Pearson wrote, "Many people will be watching the primary vote for governor for 'straws in the wind' on the segregation issue."[8]

1. Florida Political Survey Poll, Final Bulletin, April 29, 1956, in Joe Abrams file, Misc. 1956, Collins Papers.
2. Ross Beiler telephone poll report, Misc. 1956, Collins Papers. Actually, Collins carried Dade by 72 per cent.
3. John McDermott, "Warren Clobbered As Governor Runs Away from Field," *Miami Herald*, May 9, 1956, sec. G, p. 3.
4. McDermott, "Collins May Win Upset in Jacksonville."
5. McDermott, "It Looks Like LeRoy Collins Day in Florida Tuesday"; McDermott, "Adlai-Estes Choice Now Is Dangerous," *Miami Herald*, April 15, 1956, sec. G, p. 3; and McDermott, "1,000,000 Votes Tuesday in Florida," *Miami Herald*, May 7, 1956, sec. A, p. 2.
6. *New York Times*, May 6, 1956, p. 52.
7. As quoted in *Miami Herald*, May 7, 1956, sec. B, p. 3.
8. Drew Pearson, "Would Be a Modern Caesar," *Miami Herald*, April 22, 1956, sec. G, p. 2.

On May 8, Collins won in the first primary, the first such victory since the run-off system was reintroduced in 1932. The primary featured the largest registration and vote in Florida history. There were 1,277,022 registered Democrats.[9] Of these, 840,083 had voted, compared to 666,360 in 1954 and 738,497 in 1952.[10] Collins received 434,274 votes, Lowry 179,019, Bryant 110,469, and Warren 107,990.[11] Collins won 51.7 per cent of the total vote, 14,000 more than necessary for a majority and 28,465 more than the five other candidates. He received over 50 per cent of the vote in nineteen counties, all in South Florida except for his native Leon County. The Collins vote in Dade, Broward, and Palm Beach counties was 155,306, compared with 53,895 for his three adversaries. In thirty-one South Florida counties, Collins received 61.94 per cent of the total vote. These counties cast 534,130 of the total 840,083 votes. Although the Collins percentage in the thirty-six North and West Florida counties was no more than 34.2, the total vote cast there was 305,953.

Lowry was top man in twenty-six rural counties, only four of which were in South Florida. He took 21.3 per cent of the vote, compared with 13.1 per cent for Bryant and 11.7 per cent for Warren. Bryant led in his native Marion County, and Warren in his native Calhoun as well as in four others.

The real surprises of the voting were the very light vote for Warren and the size of the vote received by Bryant. The results in Duval County were also unexpected, with Collins receiving 38.1 per cent. Warren had been expected to do better than 20.7 in his former hometown in comparison to Bryant's 20.3 per cent and Lowry's 19.6.[12] There was considerable wonder at the heavy majority which Collins received in Hillsborough, Lowry's home territory, where the latter garnered only 23.3 per cent of the vote instead of an expected majority.[13]

To a very great extent the Collins vote represented a rural-urban cleavage as well as a sectional one. Collins did better than his 34 per cent average in all but one of the North or West Flor-

9. Florida, Secretary of State, Report, 1955–56, p. 326.
10. Morris, The Florida Handbook, 1957 ed., pp. 291, 292.
11. Florida Primary Elections, comp. from official canvass by R. A. Gray, Secretary of State.
12. Charles Hesser, "Appeal for Unity Issued by Victor," Miami News, May 9, 1956, sec. A, p. 1.
13. Florida Times Union, May 9, 1956, p. 24.

ida counties with large cities. However, he failed, in a number of rural South Florida counties, to equal his 61.94 South Florida average. In these, he did not average 50 per cent.

The importance of the segregation issue in influencing the voting may be viewed by considering several factors. The most significant, of course, was the 179,019 votes cast for Lowry, whose sole issue was an all-out, last-ditch stand against integration. The heavy vote Lowry received in North and West Florida was in areas where Warren had won in 1948. While some of Warren's vote there may have been alienated by the attacks on his record, it is reasonable to assume that more of it was lost because Warren failed to convince die-hard segregationists that he would stop at nothing to avoid integration. Collins' percentage of the vote in fourteen North and West Florida counties fell below even his first primary vote in 1954, although generally an incumbent governor could have been expected to increase his percentage considerably in all but the two native counties of Warren and Bryant. The huge statewide black majority for Collins was evidence of the blacks' recognition of the segregation factor. In Jacksonville, for example, the thirteen precincts with 99 per cent black registration gave Collins 9,920 votes compared with 307 for his three rivals and 496 for Peasley Streets, who espoused integration.[14] Similarly, in Miami, unofficial returns for the nine black precincts gave Collins 5,945, compared to a total of 1,312 for his adversaries. Incongruously, Lowry ran second with 709 votes.[15]

The election returns clearly indicated the cleavage in thought regarding segregation between rural and urban Florida, as well as between North Florida and the peninsula. Price, commenting on this division in *The Negro and Southern Politics*, wrote, "If the color line can only be maintained at the cost of adverse national publicity, a weakened school system, decreased business confidence, higher school bond rates and other likely results of extremist action, then that is the price that many people in North Florida are willing to pay. South Florida, which would stand to suffer the most from the repercussions of an extremist policy, may not favor desegregation, but is certainly not willing to make every sacrifice to avoid it" (pp. 95–96).

The Collins publicity emphasizing his business orientation was

14. Price, *The Negro and Southern Politics*, p. 100.
15. *Miami Herald*, May 9, 1956, sec. A, p. 2.

probably a key factor in counteracting segregation as a determinant of the primary results. However, several other factors should also be considered. Collins as the incumbent had a built-in advantage difficult for his rivals to overcome. In a state where the governor ordinarily may not succeed himself, the timing of the segregation issue for this particular year was quite important. Had Collins chosen not to run or had he been ruled ineligible, it is questionable how decisive the business issue would have been against the force of segregationist feeling. Collins' handsome appearance and agreeable personality are also factors that cannot be overlooked in an era of television, especially when contrasted with the hard, cold image presented by Lowry. Lowry's stand on a single plank until very late in the campaign certainly lost him many votes. There was unquestionably a large number of votes that went to Collins or Bryant by default from those voters who had a strong segregationist viewpoint but a more sophisticated political outlook, requiring more than a single-plank governor without previous elective experience. Warren also failed to get these votes because of his inability to impress them with his strong segregationist stand as well as his controversial record as governor. It is interesting to speculate on the political fate of a young, handsome, experienced man who presented a more constructive approach to the other state problems but also Lowry's attitudes on segregation.

Warren's defeat may be attributed to a number of factors besides those already mentioned. Estes Kefauver's presence in the state as he stumped against Stevenson served to remind people of Warren's unwillingness to cooperate with his committee.[16] The change in political techniques from whistle-stopping to television lost Warren his previous advantage over other candidates. The influx of new conservative urban voters who were unreceptive to a "Cracker" politician presenting planks like doubling the homestead exemption also contributed to his defeat.

Bryant's vote was considered quite impressive when his expenditures of $63,000 were compared with Collins' $291,000, and when his lack of organization and support were taken into account. It was assumed that he would be a "leading contender" in 1960.[17]

16. McDermott, "Estes Marks Gains While Fuller Falls."
17. *Florida Times Union,* May 20, 1956, p. 26.

According to contemporary comment, although the primary showed the profound impact made by the segregation issue, it nevertheless "definitely removed Florida from the status of extremism. . . ."[18] Ralph McGill wrote, "It was a wholesome victory for all the South."[19] Parallels were drawn between Collins' success in Florida and the almost simultaneous defeat by Lyndon Johnson of Governor Shivers in the Democratic national convention battle in Texas. The possibility was suggested that racial moderates might be in the ascendancy.[20]

The events of the years that followed failed to justify these views. Extremism became more and more prevalent in much of the South. The difficulties in Little Rock and Prince Edward County had yet to come. In Florida, the tone set by Lowry during the campaign continued with perhaps increasing overtones of racial bitterness. The significance, therefore, of a moderate in the governor's mansion became increasingly greater.

The committee appointed by Collins to study ways of maintaining segregation, with the late Judge L. L. Fabisinski of Pensacola as chairman, prepared a series of recommendations for action by the legislature. Collins called a special session of the legislature in the summer of 1956 to consider these proposals, which included a declaration of protest against the Supreme Court and an extension of the Pupil Assignment Act of 1955 to provide additional devices and procedures for delay.[21] The latter was passed the second day of the session with only Representative John Orr of Dade County voting against it.[22] A bill was also passed giving the governor emergency powers to "protect peace and tranquility."[23] Bryant assumed leadership of the die-hard segregationist faction in the House which attempted to pass more restrictive legislation. In this special session Ted David was still Speaker of the House, controlling the machinery of that body to a considerable extent. Bryant had successfully maneuvered to

18. *Miami Herald*, editorial, May 10, 1956, sec. A, p. 6.

19. Ralph McGill, "Political Story in Two States," *Miami News*, May 10, 1956, sec. A, p. 14.

20. Hendrix Chandler, "Collins-Johnson Parallels Drawn," *Florida Times Union*, May 11, 1956, p. 22.

21. Florida House of Representatives, *Journal*, Special Session, 1956, July 23, 1956, p. 7.

22. Ibid., July 24, 1956, p. 8.

23. "Floridians Debate Effectiveness of New School Laws," *Southern School News* 2 (September 1956): 13.

bring the previously tabled interposition resolution to the floor, but a fifteen-minute adjournment allowed Collins to prepare an order adjourning the entire session, preventing its passage.[24]

The 1957 legislature, presided over by Pork Chop Senator Shands and Speaker Doyle Conner from rural Bradford County, passed more extremist racial legislation. Its first act was an interposition resolution. Collins forwarded the resolution to Congress along with a message condemning it, after he had publicly branded it a "hoax."[25] The legislature seriously considered a great deal of restrictive legislation regarding segregation which Collins threatened to veto. He finally signed a bill which was intended to close any public school when federal troops were in the vicinity to enforce integration. Collins justified his signature by saying, "it is almost ridiculous to assume that any sound education could be carried on under pressure of armed guards, and as a parent, I would rather have my children at home."[26] The 1957 legislature passed the so-called last resort bill which would have authorized setting up a private school system as a last resort to prevent integration. Collins vetoed the bill, calling it the "first resort of the agitator."[27]

A conflict in attitude developed not only between the governor and the legislature, which represented the rural minority, but also between Collins and the state Supreme Court. Collins, once safely elected, said in his inaugural address, "In the first place, it will do no good whatever to defy the United States Supreme Court. Actually, this Court is an essential institution for the preservation of our form of government. It is little short of rebellion and anarchy to suggest that any state can isolate and quarantine itself against the effect of a decision of the United States Supreme Court."[28] The Florida Supreme Court refused to accept the Supreme Court order to admit blacks to Florida schools, declaring a "states rights" doctrine which was reported to be the strongest of any state court.[29]

24. Florida House of Representatives, *Journal*, August 1, 1956, pp. 154, 177.

25. *Florida Across the Threshold*, State of Florida, 1955–61.

26. "Governor Collins Signs School Closing Bill," *U.S. News and World Report* 43 (November 1, 1957): 20.

27. Florida House of Representatives, *Journal*, 1957, June 7, 1957, p. 2269.

28. "What Three Southern Governors Say About Mixing Schools," *U.S. News and World Report* 42 (January 25, 1957): 114.

29. "Conflict in Florida Position," *Southern School News* 3 (June 1957): 11.

Collins spoke before the Southern Governors Conference on "Can a Southerner Be Elected President?" He said, "The greatest danger in the South is that our people will fail to understand the change taking place around them. They must not forget that the first law of nature is change, and that the second is the survival of those who put themselves in accord with this change. This is what our Southern leadership must recognize if it expects to be listened to on the national scene. . . . If the South should wrap itself in a Confederate blanket and consume itself in racial fervor, it would surely miss its greatest opportunity for channeling into a wonderful future the products of change now taking place. And we should face up to the fact that it would bury itself politically for decades to come."[30]

Collins' attitude was clear enough when he concluded his inaugural address with a quotation from the James Russell Lowell hymn "Once to Every Man and Nation":[31]

> New occasions teach new duties
> Time makes ancient good uncouth
> They must upward still and onward
> Who would keep abreast of truth.

Lest it be thought that the Collins administration hastened forth to promote integration, it should be noted that by the end of 1960, Florida had one desegregated school district out of sixty-seven.[32] This was in Dade County, in which a school on federal property operated by the county had been desegregated. Another school, Orchard Villa, had been desegregated but became in effect another black school after only fourteen white students enrolled in September 1959. The school board installed a black faculty and admitted several hundred black children from the rapidly changing neighborhood. Two other black children were assigned to previously all-white schools in Dade in September 1960. On the university graduate level, two black women were enrolled at the University of Florida.[33] A percentage of .01 of the

30. William L. Rivers, "The Fine Art of Moderation," *Nation* 185 (December 21, 1957): 471.

31. Quoted by Ed H. Price, Jr., in foreword to LeRoy Collins, *Forerunners Courageous* (Tallahassee: Colcade Publishers, 1971), p. xiv.

32. U.S. Commission on Civil Rights, *Education 1961,* Report, Book 2, p. 238.

33. *Florida Across the Threshold,* p. 68.

total black population was attending desegregated Florida schools.[34] There had been no violence and no gubernatorial intervention.

Some violence did occur in Tallahassee. When blacks sought to desegregate the buses, riots developed. The governor, using emergency powers granted him by the 1956 legislature, suspended operation of the buses for eleven days and directed strict law enforcement to prevent violence. A compromise was reached, desegregating the buses on predominantly black runs.[35]

As late as 1960, there were still three counties in Florida with no black voting registration.[36] Collins took no known action to remedy this situation.

Collins has been criticized as a hypocrite who sold himself as a moderate to northerners while at the same time convincing southerners of his devotion to segregation. While national magazines lauded him as a leading southern moderate for his speech to the Southern Governors Conference, Governor Faubus called it "a great speech." A Collins critic wrote, "the Governor doesn't sit on the fence; he runs on it"; "The NAACP has been mollified by Governor Collins' forthright words; the White Citizens Councils can find no evidence that integration is anywhere on the horizon."[37]

On the surface, Florida remained substantially as it had been regarding the race situation. However, small changes were taking place. A major factor in this change was the Governor's Advisory Commission on Race Relations, created by the 1957 legislature at Collins' behest. In 1960, following disturbances caused by the first sit-in demonstrations, Collins appointed a successor biracial committee, known as the Fowler Commission, with Cody Fowler, former President of the American Bar Association, as its chairman. The commission had no enforcement powers, but with its professional staff and prominent membership it worked behind the scenes to ease racial tension and to prevent trouble by using the conference table approach.[38] According to one of the state's important black leaders, "the Governor's Racial Commission created

34. *Education 1961.*
35. Hendrix Chandler, "Gov. Collins Arises as Top Moderate," *Miami News,* September 25, 1957, sec. A, p. 1.
36. U.S. Commission on Civil Rights, *Voting 1961,* Report, p. 355.
37. Both quoted in Rivers, p. 471.
38. *Florida Across the Threshold,* pp. 73–83.

a racial climate in Florida that wasn't here and wouldn't have been here without it."[39]

The actions that Collins did not take are as important as his veto of the "last resort" bill, his leadership and speeches promoting tolerance and restraint, and his establishment of the biracial commission. He did not close the schools when the Orchard Villa and Air Force base schools were desegregated. He did not act to prevent blacks from attending the state universities. Florida progressed in an atmosphere of calm and order while much of the South was rocked with violence and disorder. It is difficult to judge what would have occurred if Lowry had been elected. Lowry, when questioned, replied, "I would not care to comment except to state that I would have in some way carried out my campaign pledge to the people. 'When I am elected Governor, there will be no integration of the public schools.' "[40] Perhaps what did not happen in Florida was most significant of all.

When viewed in this light, the 1956 primary was a critical one to the state. The decision was made to abstain from any action which might produce disorder. A commitment was made by the state toward an increasingly moderate racial policy from which it could turn back only with great difficulty.

39. Interview with Father Gibson.
40. Lowry letter.

Appendix

ILLUSTRATION 1.—PRIMARY EXPENDITURES

Year	Candidate	Amount spent in first primary	Amount spent in second primary	Total
1952	Dan McCarty*	$156,239	$ 95,721	$251,960
	Brailey Odham	72,753	84,616	157,369
	Alto Adams	154,401		154,401
1954	LeRoy Collins*	178,600	143,024	321,624
	Charley Johns	245,944	121,957	366,901
	Brailey Odham	146,675		146,675
1956	LeRoy Collins*	291,183		291,183
	Sumter Lowry	115,216		115,216
	Farris Bryant	63,048		63,048
	Fuller Warren	194,682		194,682

SOURCE: Price, *The Negro and Southern Politics*, p. 97.
*Winning candidate

ILLUSTRATION 2.—URBAN-RURAL MAP

Shaded portions show
urban counties

SOURCE: Havard and Beth, *The Politics of Misrepresentation*, p. 15.

ILLUSTRATION 3.—Map Showing Collins' Strength

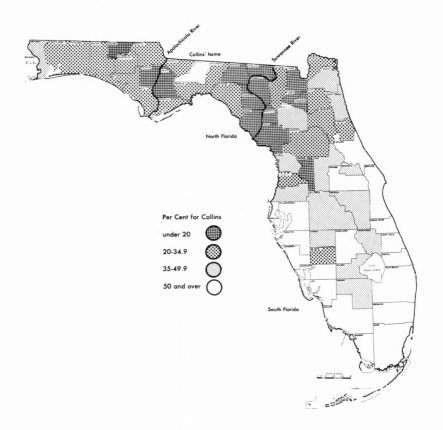

Apalachicola River

Collins' home

Suwannee River

North Florida

Per Cent for Collins

under 20

20-34.9

35-49.9

50 and over

South Florida

Price, *The Negro and Southern Politics*, p. 101.

ILLUSTRATION 4.—TABLE OF VOTING BY COUNTIES

Counties	Farris Bryant	LeRoy Collins	Sumter L. Lowry	W. B. (Bill) Price	Peaslie Streets	Fuller Warren
Alachua	3,359	5,272	2,504	73	64	1,818
Baker	494	435	1,173	14	4	690
Bay	2,066	5,166	3,632	32	11	4,018
Bradford	1,179	794	1,452	26	3	785
Brevard	1,591	5,034	1,269	16	8	512
Broward	1,731	23,858	2,994	102	67	1,848
Calhoun	95	334	461	4	5	2,439
Charlotte	220	1,366	540	14	7	284
Citrus	353	1,295	895	3	5	690
Clay	853	1,546	1,546	16	11	966
Collier	293	1,981	875	25	5	347
Columbia	1,504	1,769	2,413	21	4	1,090
Dade	7,916	112,858	18,696	1,050	2,368	13,589
De Soto	380	1,039	1,289	7	3	259
Dixie	174	335	974	13	1	347
Duval	16,996	31,761	16,391	232	816	17,221
Escambia	6,702	16,785	8,117	189	49	3,333
Flagler	274	346	500	14	2	151
Franklin	169	832	1,002	9	14	503
Gadsden	777	1,171	920		2	1,423
Gilchrist	198	169	662	4	1	257
Glades	66	408	383		3	55
Gulf	173	880	1,177	9	5	879
Hamilton	544	438	1,170	10	3	466
Hardee	460	1,442	1,629	17	2	563
Hendry	176	1,306	1,239	8	2	133
Hernando	199	810	915	2	8	1,277
Highlands	463	3,008	1,287	8	4	421
Hillsborough	5,425	35,615	14,426	181	612	5,716
Holmes	389	700	2,924	31	9	1,391
Indian River	481	2,305	463	5	7	1,010
Jackson	681	2,470	3,347	33	20	3,824
Jefferson	328	578	1,031	1	2	520
Lafayette	217	194	935	7	1	337
Lake	3,329	5,288	3,007	16	9	1,491
Lee	2,241	5,384	1,824	24	13	808
Leon	1,451	8,863	992	13	26	3,653
Levy	585	627	1,702	13		793
Liberty	83	129	770	11	5	434
Madison	1,175	771	1,789	19	7	415
Manatee	1,726	6,965	2,407	23	8	1,041
Marion	6,349	3,216	1,419	37	15	1,023
Martin	212	2,904	767	3	15	263
Monroe	462	4,371	782	122	17	837
Nassau	1,357	1,556	1,167	28	7	1,004
Okaloosa	977	3,103	4,261	53	15	1,687
Okeechobee	67	686	721	3	1	334
Orange	6,311	17,740	5,302	67	56	1,851
Osceola	845	2,084	1,256	11	6	337
Palm Beach	2,347	18,590	6,084	84	140	1,891
Pasco	495	2,905	2,484	19	19	883
Pinellas	4,027	23,710	3,649	102	83	3,155
Polk	4,153	16,752	10,676	55	52	2,963
Putnam	1,622	2,056	2,367	17	3	1,398
St. Johns	1,742	3,990	2,520	30	18	763
St. Lucie	653	4,669	1,241	22	13	1,118
Santa Rosa	757	2,133	3,483	19	10	1,367
Sarasota	601	4,512	817	48	113	510
Seminole	1,773	3,598	1,462	12	16	496
Sumter	856	796	1,782	6	3	556
Suwannee	1,074	784	2,844	7	2	511
Taylor	387	876	1,946	17	2	657
Union	237	91	468	4	2	961
Volusia	4,532	17,542	4,292	146	252	2,116
Wakulla	216	486	686	6	5	874
Walton	458	1,663	2,732	20	21	1,394
Washington	443	1,134	2,089	12	4	1,244
	110,469	434,274	179,019	3,245	5,086	107,990
Total						840,083

SOURCE: Florida Secretary of State, Florida Primary Elections 1956.

UNIVERSITY OF FLORIDA MONOGRAPHS

Social Sciences

1. *The Whigs of Florida, 1845–1854,* by Herbert J. Doherty, Jr.

2. *Austrian Catholics and the Social Question, 1918–1933,* by Alfred Diamant

3. *The Siege of St. Augustine in 1702,* by Charles W. Arnade

4. *New Light on Early and Medieval Japanese Historiography,* by John A. Harrison

5. *The Swiss Press and Foreign Affairs in World War II,* by Frederick H. Hartmann

6. *The American Militia: Decade of Decision, 1789–1800,* by John K. Mahon

7. *The Foundation of Jacques Maritain's Political Philosophy,* by Hwa Yol Jung

8. *Latin American Population Studies,* by T. Lynn Smith

9. *Jacksonian Democracy on the Florida Frontier,* by Arthur W. Thompson

10. *Holman Versus Hughes: Extension of Australian Commonwealth Powers,* by Conrad Joyner

11. *Welfare Economics and Subsidy Programs,* by Milton Z. Kafoglis

12. *Tribune of the Slavophiles: Konstantin Aksakov,* by Edward Chmielewski

13. *City Managers in Politics: An Analysis of Manager Tenure and Termination,* by Gladys M. Kammerer, Charles D. Farris, John M. DeGrove, and Alfred B. Clubok

14. *Recent Southern Economic Development as Revealed by the Changing Structure of Employment,* by Edgar S. Dunn, Jr.

15. *Sea Power and Chilean Independence,* by Donald E. Worcester

16. *The Sherman Antitrust Act and Foreign Trade,* by Andre Simmons

17. *The Origins of Hamilton's Fiscal Policies,* by Donald F. Swanson

18. *Criminal Asylum in Anglo-Saxon Law,* by Charles H. Riggs, Jr.

19. *Colonia Barón Hirsch, A Jewish Agricultural Colony in Argentina,* by Morton D. Winsberg

20. *Time Deposits in Present-Day Commercial Banking,* by Lawrence L. Crum

21. *The Eastern Greenland Case in Historical Perspective,* by Oscar Svarlien

22. *Jacksonian Democracy and the Historians,* by Alfred A. Cave

23. *The Rise of the American Chemistry Profession, 1850–1900,* by Edward H. Beardsley

24. *Aymara Communities and the Bolivian Agrarian Reform,* by William E. Carter

25. *Conservatives in the Progressive Era: The Taft Republicans of 1912,* by Norman M. Wilensky

26. *The Anglo-Norwegian Fisheries Case of 1951 and the Changing Law of the Territorial Sea,* by Teruo Kobayashi

27. *The Liquidity Structure of Firms and Monetary Economics,* by William J. Frazer, Jr.

28. *Russo-Persian Commercial Relations, 1828–1914,* by Marvin L. Entner

29. *The Imperial Policy of Sir Robert Borden,* by Harold A. Wilson

30. *The Association of Income and Educational Achievement,* by Roy L. Lassiter, Jr.

31. *Relation of the People to the Land in Southern Iraq,* by Fuad Baali

32. *The Price Theory of Value in Public Finance,* by Donald R. Escarraz

33. *The Process of Rural Development in Latin America,* by T. Lynn Smith

34. *To Be or Not to Be . . . Existential-Psychological Perspectives on the Self,* edited by Sidney M. Jourard

35. *Politics in a Mexican Community,* by Lawrence S. Graham

36. *A Two-Sector Model of Economic Growth with Technological Progress,* by Frederick Owen Goddard

37. *Florida Studies in the Helping Professions,* by Arthur W. Combs

38. *The Ancient Synagogues of the Iberian Peninsula,* by Don A. Halperin

39. *An Estimate of Personal Wealth in Oklahoma in 1960,* by Richard Edward French

40. *Congressional Oversight of Executive Agencies,* by Thomas A. Henderson

41. *Historians and Meiji Statesmen,* by Richard T. Chang

42. *Welfare Economics and Peak Load Pricing: A Theoretical Application to Municipal Water Utility Practices,* by Robert Lee Greene

43. *Factor Analysis in International Relations: Interpretation, Problem Areas, and an Application,* by Jack E. Vincent

44. *The Sorcerer's Apprentice: The French Scientist's Image of German Science, 1840–1919,* by Harry W. Paul

45. *Community Power Structure: Propositional Inventory, Tests, and Theory,* by Claire W. Gilbert

46. *Human Capital, Technology, and the Role of the United States in International* Trade, by John F. Morrall III

47. *The Segregation Factor in the Florida Democratic Gubernatorial Primary of 1956, by* Helen L. Jacobstein